RSPB

POCKET BIRDFEEDER

HANDBOOK

POCKET
BIRDFEEDER
HANDBOOK

ROBERT BURTON

PHOTOGRAPHY
KIM TAYLOR

DORLING KINDERSLEY
LONDON • NEW YORK • SYDNEY • MOSCOW

A Dorling Kindersley Book

Art Editor Caroline Murray
Project Editor Roger Smoothy

First published in Great Britain in 1990
by Dorling Kindersley Limited,
9 Henrietta Street, London WC2E 8PS

First pocket edition published 1997

8 10 9

The material in this book was previously published under the title of
RSPB Birdfeeder Handbook

A CIP catalogue record for this book is available
from the British Library

ISBN 0 7513 0413 1

Reproduction by Colourscan, Singapore
Printed and bound in Italy by Lego

CONTENTS

•

CHAPTER ONE

ATTRACTING BIRDS

A GARDEN WILL BE visited by birds only
if it offers some of the necessities of life.
Every bird needs three fundamental things for
its well-being – food, water and shelter. If some
of these basics can be found in the garden,
they make a visit worthwhile and increase
the birds' chances of survival. You cannot
guarantee that these provisions will be naturally
available in your garden, but there are many
ways that you can artificially reproduce them.
Putting out food on bird-tables, filling a bird-
bath with water and providing nest-boxes for
roosting and nesting all create a bird-friendly
environment. This chapter describes birdfeeders
(together with the food to put on them) as well
as bird-baths and nest-boxes that you can
either make or buy. Hints on their construction
and use will help you improve your
garden with birds in mind.

A blue tit appreciating a bird-bath

∴ WHAT BIRDS NEED ∴

Your success in attracting birds depends on how closely you can fulfil their basic needs. Even if your garden does not contain a natural wealth of food, a water supply or large, mature trees for nest sites, you can still copy these features in the garden by providing food, birdfeeders, bird-baths and nest-boxes. Knocking together pieces of wood for nest-boxes and birdfeeders provides the chance to satisfy a creative, do-it-yourself urge. Moreover, they are a great place to start for the novice woodworker. The birds will not mind if the construction is less than perfect, and only a little practice and application is needed to solve the Christmas present problem. Your efforts will not take you long and will be quickly appreciated.

• FEEDING THE BIRDS •

Feeding the birds is a pastime that ranges from casually throwing crusts out of the kitchen window to distributing commercial quantities of food in a battery of feeding devices. Food you provide for birds not

Squirrel menace
Frustrate squirrels by using a hanging feeder with holes that do not allow anything larger than a small bird to pass inside.

only keeps them well fed but also reduces the amount of energy they have to spend searching for a meal. This can be important in the winter cold or when there are young to feed in summer.

The amount of money and effort you put into feeding birds depends on your level of interest and the time you can devote to watching them. My birdfeeder array is strategically positioned outside my study window and, to provide a welcome distraction from work, I ensure that there is always enough food throughout the day to keep the birds coming. Furthermore, I am making some systematic studies of who uses the bird-table, so I have every excuse to gaze out of the window.

New stainless steel feeder
Designed to attract a wide range of small birds. The feeder holds over 900 g (2 lb) of peanuts.

· WINTER FOOD ·

It is often said that once you start putting out food for birds in winter, you should not stop until spring arrives, and that if you cannot guarantee a continuous supply, it is best not to start at all. This strikes me as rather strict and unnecessary. While birdfeeders make life much easier for birds and contribute to their survival in hard times, no bird relies entirely on one food source. In natural circumstances, birds have to adapt to changing food stocks and their livelihood depends on quickly finding new supplies.

Yet there are two situations in which birds may become dependent on birdfeeders. In unusually harsh spells, when natural food is unobtainable, well-stocked birdfeeders are definite life-savers. As these periods do not last long, there is no need to provide supplies for months. And on large, new housing estates, especially where gardens are still rather bare, feeders help maintain a high population. Birds do not feed only in one garden: they have regular rounds through a neighbourhood, so if you are away on a holiday, the birds will simply bypass the empty bird-table until your return.

However, where feeders have been maintaining an unnaturally high population, a shortage of food could develop if the birds were forced back on to natural supplies, especially at the end of winter when stocks are low. I suspect that we simply do not know enough about the winter feeding habits of garden birds to make a strict ruling, but do not feel guilty if your feeders remain empty for a while.

Hopper *Even in winter, nuts* (left) *go uncollected if there is enough natural food available.*

Food source *A tit-bell* (right) *is a life-saver in hard times.*

· SUMMER FOOD ·

Many people stop feeding their birds in summer when some interesting birds, such as siskins and fieldfares, migrate to their breeding-grounds and others return to the countryside to nest. Those that remain tend to switch to natural foods and ignore the bird-table but, the garden cannot be relied upon to be a good source of food. If you have coaxed tits and others to nest in your garden by putting up

Summer scraps *Persuade a robin to stay in your garden over summer by continuing to place out food for it in a feeding bowl.*

Log-feeder *Food in summer (above) is appreciated by birds that stay in the garden.*

Scrap basket *Resume putting out supplies of food, such as bread and cheese (right), after the young birds have left the nest.*

nest-boxes, it is reasonable to make sure that their families will have enough to eat. The danger is that the nestlings may by fed unsuitable food, although some birds give their nestlings a different diet from their own anyway so they can still feed at the bird-table while finding natural food for their offspring. The problems come when natural food is scarce and the nestlings are stuffed with dry bread, coconut or peanuts, which can easily choke them. If you stop putting out food during nesting, do start again when the fledglings appear. They will benefit from easy meals and you may have the pleasure of seeing entire families of tits, nuthatches and even woodpeckers together at a birdfeeder.

• WATER •

Pause to reflect *A marsh tit perches on the rim of a bird-bath before taking a drink.*

Birds need water for both drinking and bathing. Those species that feed on worms, caterpillars and other juicy animals do not need to drink as much as birds that live exclusively on a diet of dry seeds, but a supply of water is always welcome. Putting a bird-bath in your garden is another incentive for birds to visit because water is required all year round.

The bird-bath is very popular during hot summer weather when birds need to keep cool and when puddles and pools have dried up in the drought. Birds do not sweat as we do but pant to keep cool, rather like dogs, by evaporating water from their mouths and lungs. However, contrary to popular assumption, birds use the bird-bath more frequently in winter than in summer because it becomes a vital reservoir of drinking water when frequent frosts seal off natural supplies.

You can sometimes see birds taking mouthfuls of snow to get water but this is rather like eating ice cream in a blizzard. It takes 12 times as much heat to melt a gram of ice as it does to warm the same amount of water to body heat. So just keeping the bird-bath clear of ice will help the birds at a time when saving energy is so important. Birds also like to bathe in frosty weather because they must maintain their plumage in peak condition to keep warm. If birds cannot find water, both their flight efficiency and insulation will be impaired. This will cost them dearly in wasted energy.

· NEST SITES ·

Even in a mature garden that is well stocked with trees, dense climbers or shrubs, there is likely to be a shortage of suitable nest sites. This is especially true if large numbers of local birds have been maintained through the winter by free handouts at birdfeeders.

A few birds will nest in hidden corners and raise families. Nest-boxes bring more birds into the garden and make it easier for you to follow the unfolding saga of birds' family lives, while the birds' investment of time and energy is less likely to end in disaster. Although some birds, especially the finches, never use nest-boxes, hole-nesters, such as tits and starlings, eagerly accept them.

The nest-box must be sited at least 1.8 m (6 ft) above the ground, away from the worst effects of the sun and rain, for

Metal plate (right) *If there is a danger of squirrels and woodpeckers enlarging a tit-box entrance, nail a metal plate around the hole.*

example, under a tree canopy. It should be secure enough not to fall down, but it does not matter if it wobbles a little.

Resist the temptation to visit the nest-box too often – the laying period is a particularly sensitive time. If nestlings are disturbed when they are well-grown, they are likely to "explode" out of the nest. If they do, gently prod them back into the box and stuff the hole with a handkerchief until they settle down.

Timing *Put up your nest-box before New Year: this allows it to weather and gives early-pairing birds a chance to inspect it and roost there.*

∵ BIRD-TABLES AND FEEDERS ∵

T HERE IS A WIDE variety of birdfeeding devices on the market,
suitable for all kinds of taste and garden situation. Making
your own is much more satisfying, and few tools and little skill
are needed to turn out acceptable products. Birdfeeders bring
birds to eye-level, giving you the opportunity to observe all the
birds' excitement as they jostle for food. Site the feeder out
of full sun and in a sheltered location, preferably near suitable
perches. Take care to place the feeder away from cover where
cats can wait in ambush. Add a low roof to prevent rain
sweeping away the food. When building the birdfeeders,
follow either the metric or imperial measurements given
below: it is not possible to swap between the two.

· OPEN BIRD-TABLE ·

The open bird-table is the traditional way
to provide food for birds. It is easy to
make, consisting of a board held up on
a post or hung from a branch or bracket
with chains. Use the dimensions for the
floor of the covered bird-table (shown
opposite). Cut the base of the tray from

a sheet of 12 mm (½ in) plywood and
make the rim from lengths of 20 mm
(¾ in) square wood. Fix these side pieces
with 30 mm (1¼ in) nails. Reduce the
chance of squirrels reaching the table by
attaching an inverted biscuit tin or conical
piece of metal near the top of the post.

Low rim *The surrounding edges help to prevent
food being scattered, but leave gaps at the
corners to let rainwater drain away.*

Screw

Feeding tray
*For ground-
feeders, such as
wrens, support the
tray on short legs.*

Wooden blocks
*Nail small blocks
to the centre of the
underside of the tray
to make a seating for
the supporting post.*

Post *Support the tray on top
of a post, about 1.5 m (5 ft)
in length. Make the post
from smooth wood (or use
a galvanized iron pole)
and attach the anti-predator
devices. Firmly drive the post
in and then screw on the table
through the blocks.*

Hook

Log-feeder
*To entertain
woodpeckers,
nuthatches
and tits (p.10)
hang a log-
feeder from
your bird-
table.*

Holes
*Drill holes
through the
log and stuff
them with fat.*

·COVERED BIRD-TABLE·

Once you have made an open bird-table it is quite simple to add a roof, which keeps the food dry and provides a place for a hanging seed hopper. Make the roof from 9 mm (^{3}/8 in) ply and angle one long edge of each roof piece. Cut the uprights from 20 mm (^{3}/4 in) square wood: angle both ends of each upright by sawing off wedges, 4 mm (^{1}/8 in) from the bottom and 6 mm (^{1}/4 in) from the top.

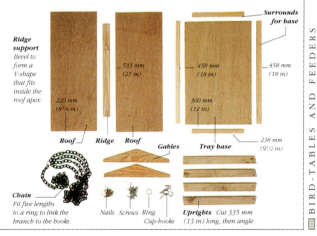

Cup-hooks

Gables
Cut triangular shapes, 300 mm (12 in) wide and 60 mm (2^1/2 in) tall. Fix to the uprights, then screw in the ridge.

Assembly Nail the uprights to the inside corners of the tray. The uprights will not be vertical – they should slant slightly outwards. Attach the gables and fit in the ridge. Fasten on the roof pieces, making sure the angled edges fit together at the apex.

Hanging table
Screw four cup-hooks through the corners of the roof and into the gable ends. Hang from a branch on chains. The table can also be fixed on a post.

Front view

Ridge support
Bevel to form a V-shape that fits inside the roof apex.

220 mm (8^3/8 in)

533 mm (21 in)

458 mm (18 in)

458 mm (18 in)

300 mm (12 in)

Surrounds for base

238 mm (9^1/2 in)

Roof   **Ridge**   **Roof**   **Gables**   **Tray base**

Chain
Fit five lengths to a ring to link the branch to the hooks.

Nails   *Screws*   *Ring*   *Cup-hooks*

Uprights *Cut 335 mm (13 in) long, then angle.*

13

· BIRD PUDDING HOLDER ·

If you decide to make your bird pudding (p.22) in an old food tin, you can either directly turn the pudding out on to the bird-table or else simply build a special holder for the tin. The holder, which can be nailed to a post or tree trunk, not only keeps the bird pudding dry but also guarantees that it lasts longer because it is not so easy for birds to break off and carry away large chunks. The small screws that fasten the tin in place can easily be removed to release the tin, so it can be refilled with bird pudding. To ensure the top edge of the tin is not jagged or sharp, and does not cut the birds, use a tin opener that leaves a smooth, blunt edge. This feeder holds a 450 g (1 lb) tin; if you use a tin of a different size adjust the dimensions given below accordingly. Cut out the pieces of wood from 20 mm (¾ in) thick floorboard or plywood.

Steadying brace
The base of the brace is 125 mm (5 in) long, and is notched to fit over the can.

Hole *Allows holder to be nailed to a tree*

Front view *The tin can is secured in position between the two side supports by the 15 mm (⅝ in) screws.*

94 mm
(3⅛ in)

Side support

225 mm
(9 in)

150 mm
(6 in)

Drilled holes

Back

125 mm
(5 in)

Side support

Side view

Assembly Mark the position of the side supports on the back piece, and drill holes for the four long screws. Fix on the sides by screwing through the back and nail on the steadying brace. Fit the tin between supports. Make a pilot hole in each of the side pieces to take the small screws. Turn the screws until they hold the tin in place.

Rust-proof screws 60 mm (2½ in)

Empty tin can

Screws 15 mm (⅝ in)

Oval nails 30 mm (1¼ in)

• SCRAP BASKET •

A scrap basket filled with kitchen left-overs (pp.18–19) or various nuts (p.23) is appreciated by many different birds. The simplest container is a netting bag that stops scraps being blown about, but the food soon becomes sodden and the bag messy. It is quite easy to make a refillable basket that will keep the food dry. Use galvanized wire or plastic-coated mesh to cover the front and base of the basket; 20 mm (³/₄ in) floorboard for the sides, back, brace and batten; and 12 mm (¹/₂ in) ply for the lid. Attach the lid with a 105 mm (4¹/₈ in) length of piano hinge.

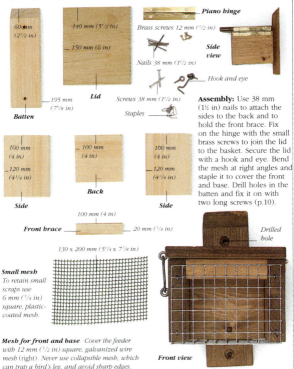

60 mm (2¹/₂ in)

140 mm (5¹/₂ in)

150 mm (6 in)

195 mm (7⁷/₈ in)

Lid

Batten

Piano hinge

Brass screws 12 mm (¹/₂ in)

Side view

Nails 38 mm (1¹/₂ in)

Hook and eye

Screws 38 mm (1¹/₂ in)

Staples

100 mm (4 in)

120 mm (4³/₄ in)

Side

100 mm (4 in)

Back

100 mm (4 in)

120 mm (4³/₄ in)

Side

Assembly: Use 38 mm (1½ in) nails to attach the sides to the back and to hold the front brace. Fix on the hinge with the small brass screws to join the lid to the basket. Secure the lid with a hook and eye. Bend the mesh at right angles and staple it to cover the front and base. Drill holes in the batten and fix it on with two long screws (p.10).

100 mm (4 in)

Front brace

20 mm (³/₄ in)

130 x 200 mm (5¹/₄ x 7⁷/₈ in)

Drilled hole

Small mesh
To retain small scraps use 6 mm (¹/₄ in) square, plastic-coated mesh.

Mesh for front and base Cover the feeder with 12 mm (¹/₂ in) square, galvanized wire mesh (right). Never use collapsible mesh, which can trap a bird's leg, and avoid sharp edges.

Front view

•SEED HOPPER•

A hopper is the most practical way to provide seeds as it keeps them dry and stops the wind blowing them away. Other methods tend to be wasteful, although ground-feeding birds, such as chaffinches and dunnocks, prefer their seeds broadcast on the lawn. This hopper, which uses a 450 g (1 lb) jam jar, is simple to make. Using the dimensions given (altering as necessary for a different jar size), cut the base from 25 mm (1 in) wood, the side surrounds from 20 mm (³/₄ in) square wood and the back from 12 mm (¹/₂ in) plywood. When the hopper is built, fill the jar with seeds, or nuts, and invert it. (Cover the jar with a piece of card to prevent spillage while you are fitting it into place.) You can adjust the height of the jar above the tray to regulate the flow of different sizes of seed.

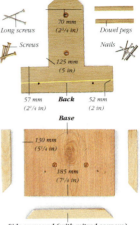

Back
70 mm (2³/₄ in)
125 mm (5 in)
57 mm (2¹/₄ in)   52 mm (2 in)

Long screws   *Dowel pegs*
Screws   *Nails*

Base
130 mm (5¹/₄ in)
185 mm (7¹/₄ in)

Side surround (with mitred corners)

Webbing and tacks

Jam jar

Back piece
When the hopper is completed, tack both ends of the webbing to the back piece. Fix the hopper to a tree trunk through two holes drilled in the back.

Gaps *Leave gaps in the surround for water drainage.*

Front view

Dowel pegs
Two wooden pegs steady the jar.

Elastic webbing
Secure the jar with webbing that allows it to be removed for refilling.

Assembly Fix the back on to the base using the long screws. Then, nail on the side surrounds, leaving gaps at the corners. Drill two holes in the base to take the 80 mm (3¹/₈ in) long dowels. Screw three small screws under the rim of the jar to raise it off the base and let seeds fall out. To alter the size of the gap, turn the screws either clockwise or anti-clockwise.

· WINDOW FEEDER ·

You do not need a garden to attract birds. Use this feeder, which attaches to a window-sill, to see the entertaining activity of the bird-table at close quarters. Even in built-up areas you can at least rely on blackbirds, starlings and sparrows to pay a visit. The window feeder combines three different types of feeder. The feeding tray (p.12) has a narrow, oblong-shaped base to fit along the width of the window. The design of the scrap basket (p.15) has been slightly modified: a wedge-shaped basket, of the same width as the feeding tray, leaves more space on the tray. Cover the front of the basket with mesh and hinge the lid. The seed hopper (p.16) has been altered because its separate base is unnecessary. The jar is held by a datachable webbing strap, to enable the jar to be refilled easily. Two blocks nailed on to the back piece replace the dowels.

Wedge-shaped scrap basket

Seed hopper *The jar is fixed with detachable webbing, secured by a small peg.*

Attachment to the window-sill
Hook the feeder to the sill so that one side of the table is against the front edge of the sill and the back of the bracket rests against the wall.

Side view

Hanging the feeder *Build a bracket to support the feeder. To make a rigid fixing, extend the bracket under the sill so that it is braced against the wall. Screw hooks into the front edge of the sill and eyes to match in the side of the tray that faces the window.*

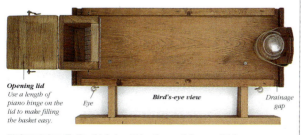

Opening lid
Use a length of piano hinge on the lid to make filling the basket easy.

Eye

Bird's-eye view

Drainage gap

Kitchen window-sill *Place this feeder outside the kitchen window and then you can simply throw out leftovers and kitchen scraps to tempt many different kinds of bird.*

∴ BIRD-TABLE FARE ∴

· KITCHEN SCRAPS ·

BIRDS NEED FOODS RICH in carbohydrates and fats to help them build up the vital reserves of body fat that they need to survive long, cold nights. Many kitchen scraps have a high fat content and are ideal bird food – suet, bone marrow, dripping, stale cheese, bacon rind, cake and pastry. However, to avoid the possible spread of diseases, only put out bones and meat that have been cooked. (Always ensure that poultry bones are out of the reach of cats or dogs.) Never give birds desiccated coconut or uncooked rice as these can swell up inside the bird, often with fatal results. For this reason it is also best to soak dry bread in water before leaving it out on the bird-table.

Stale cake

Crusts and crumbs
Bread is the food most often put out for birds. It is not the best choice as it is not very nutritious but, as with humans, it helps fill empty stomachs. Stale cake and broken pieces from the bottom of the biscuit tin are more suitable as they are rich in fat. Put out fine crumbs for shy species, such as dunnocks and wrens.

Breadcrumbs and crusts

Broken biscuit

Cooked potatoes Potatoes in their jackets, which have been split open, last well as the soft contents can only be carried away a beakful at a time, and the skins take a long time to pick clean.

Uncooked pastry

Cooked spaghetti

Rice, pasta and pastry
Leftovers of cooked rice and spaghetti, and any uncooked pastry remains from your baking, are all rich in starch and will keep starlings and rooks busy.

Jacket potato

Cooked rice

Fruit In late summer, fruit attracts birds as well as butterflies, bees and wasps. Gather some of the windfalls in autumn and store them in a cool, dark place. In the dead of winter, when birds have exhausted the natural supplies of fruit and berries, put the windfalls on the lawn, together with fruit you have bought that is past its prime. Or else, cut the fruit into pieces or impale it on spikes on the bird-table. Blackbirds, fieldfares, redwings, starlings and smaller birds such as black-caps, robins and blue tits all enjoy fruit.

Apple

Pear

Stale cheese

Dry Cheese Cheese that has dried out and become hard is ideal for birds, although the blue varieties and strongly flavoured ones tend to be left. For smaller species, such as the goldcrest, crumble or grate the cheese into little pieces. In cold weather, wrens, which do not visit the bird table, appreciate cheese crumbs sprinkled among leaf litter. Stale cheese also makes an excellent ingredient of bird pudding.

Fat and meat Put lumps of fat, bacon rind or fat trimmed off chops on to the bird-table. Melt large lumps of fat or dripping to pour over branches or into a log-feeder (p.12) or tit-bell. Hang cooked lumps of meat or meat bones, with shreds of meat and fat attached, to attract tits, starlings and woodpeckers as well as members of the crow family. Catfood is a gourmet food for birds!

Bacon rinds

Tinned catfood

Lard/cooking fat

Marrow bone

Meat bone

·GRAIN AND SEEDS·

GRAIN AND SEEDS PROVIDE birds with a valuable source of fats, carbohydrates, oils, minerals and vitamins. Some birds, such as the greenfinch and chaffinch, will eat almost any seeds from large cereal grains to small weed seeds, although sunflower seeds are the most popular of all. Other birds are more fastidious: siskins, for example, are particularly fond of niger seeds, whereas inches, tits and even pipits are attracted to hemp seeds. Pet shops sell ready-made seed mixes, which have been specially formulated to satisfy the appetites and nutritional needs of a wide variety of birds, but you can easily make up your own mixes at a much reduced cost. You can buy the grain and seeds individually and even supplement the mix with wild seeds (dock, thistle, stinging nettle, knapweed, teazel and ragwort) collected from the garden and dried. To avoid too much spillage serve the mixes from a seed hopper (p.16).

Popping corn This cereal grain is a useful source of oil and starch.

Pot barley The barley grain has a high bran, germ and vitamin content.

Wheat grain The whole grain is best as it contains valuable vitamins, minerals and fat, as well as fibre.

Rolled oats Oats are rich in protein and fats, but serve rolled oats as birds cannot easily remove the tough husks.

Hemp seeds These seeds are a favourite among tits and nuthatches, which hammer the seeds to crack them open.

Niger seeds Rich in oil, niger seeds come from the ramtil plant, which is cultivated in India.

Millet seeds These grass seeds have a high starch content and are a good source of minerals and vitamins.

Sunflower seeds A great bird food, sunflower seeds are very nutritious, being full of oil, protein and minerals.

Wild bird seeds This commercially available mixture contains a large range of seeds and grains that attracts larger birds.

Canary seed mix A proprietary mix, rich in canary seed, linseed, hemp and black rape, is suitable for small species of bird.

· MAKING FOOD ·

IT IS EASY TO PREPARE food that brings birds to the bird-
table. Bird pudding is quick to make and is an ideal way
to use up kitchen scraps (although uncooked vegetables should
not be included). Melt shredded suet, cooking fat or dripping in
a pan to bind the pudding. It is generally unwise to give birds
any food that is highly seasoned or strongly salted. Peanuts are
very nutritious and they can be hung up on string, galvanized
wire or in a mesh bag to attract a large number of birds. Make
sure to buy high-quality peanuts that have been approved as
bird food. Rearing your own mealworms requires a little more
work but it is well worthwhile as robins may become hand-
tame to take these delicacies. Mealworms are mobile and
so should be served in a deep dish.

Seed pudding

Shredded suet

Fat ball

Suet stick

Nut pudding

Bird pudding You can either buy fat balls
and suet sticks or make your own bird
puddings. Half fill a tit-bell, coconut shell
or tin (p.14) with a mixture of seeds, nuts,
sultanas, cheese crumbs and cake scraps
and then stir in almost the same amount
of melted suet or fat to bind it. Allow the
mixture to set solid before putting it out.

Mealworms The grubs, sold in pet
shops, can be reared in a container
filled with layers of bran and biscuit
or dried bread. Keep the contents
warm and just moist. The grubs
pupate into beetles, which then lay
eggs that hatch after about a week
into more grubs. In a few weeks
you will have a self-sustaining
colony from which you can pick
or sieve a crop of mealworms.

Tin box A pierced lid
lets the grubs breathe.

Mealworms These are
larvae of a common
brown beetle.

Fresh, half-coconut

Peanuts in their shells, strung on a galvanized wire

Red mesh bag

Fruit and nuts A fresh, half-coconut, hung upside-down, is a great favourite of tits. Birds love all kinds of nut – for most species the nuts should be opened to allow the birds to get at the kernels but woodpeckers and nuthatches can hammer shells apart. Nuts disappear quickly from feeders as birds take them away to hoard. Chop nuts to attract smaller species. Dried fruit can be added to bird pudding or, after soaking, placed on the bird-table.

Peanuts

Peanuts Because of their high fat and protein content, peanuts are a useful bird food. Thread peanuts in their shells on thin wire or string for tits, or put shelled, unsalted nuts in a mesh bag or wire container to attract greenfinches and other birds. In summer, grate whole nuts to prevent nestlings choking.

Hazelnuts

Chopped nuts

Almonds

Walnuts

Raisins, sultanas and currants

Dried apricots

∴ BIRD-BATHS AND PONDS ∴·

THE BIRD-BATH IS a useful accessory to the birdfeeder array, because the resource of water is as necessary for birds as food. Birds come to the bird-bath throughout the year both to drink and bathe, while members of the crow family dunk hard food in the water to soften it. Bathing helps maintain the plumage and, in summer, keeps birds cool. Watching the activity at the bird-bath is entertaining and you will be able to identify several different species. Starlings and sparrows are the most frequent users and, as at the bird-table, these sociable birds crowd together around the water. Other regular visitors include blackbirds, blue tits, greenfinches, chaffinches, wrens and collared doves, but the bird-bath may also attract rarer birds, such as redpolls, hawfinches and crossbills.

· BIRD-BATHS ·

Sundial An expensive bath with a sundial has a classical feel, but it is no more likely to attract birds.

There are many kinds of purpose-built bird-baths available from garden centres and pet shops, catering for different tastes. Some designs are more ornamental than practical. From a bird's point of view there are two major considerations: the bird-bath should have gently sloping sides, to allow small birds to paddle in and out easily, and a rough surface, so they can get a safe footing. Ideally, the bath should have a "deep end", 8–9 cm (3–3¹⁄₂ in) deep, which is large enough for a pigeon to soak itself or a flock of starlings to have a good splash without emptying all the water out of the bath.

You may be able to find a cheaper substitute in a hardware shop or you can easily make your own. An upside-down,

Cheap baths Terracotta flower pot bases are ideal.

Bath-time A wren splashes about in a bath.

galvanized dustbin lid, propped up on bricks, is often quoted as making an acceptable bird-bath, but the metal surface may be too slippery. Large dishes and flower pot bases are also possibilities. If the shape of container does not allow for both shallow and deep water, make an island from a stone. Alternatively, you can mould a simple and presentable bird-bath from mortar. Improvise the pedestal from a 7.5 cm (3 in) drainpipe or a pre-formed concrete post. Site the bird-bath near a tree where the birds can retire to dry and preen in safety. An ornamental bird-bath may well look attractive as a feature in the centre of the garden but this is usually not the best position for it.

MAKING A SIMPLE BIRD-BATH

Cut out a strip of hardboard. Nail the ends to a wooden block to form a girdle. Pour the mortar mix into the girdle. As it sets, shape it with a board or metal plate to form a shallow dish. Fix the bird-bath to a pedestal or lay it on the lawn.

· WATER IN WINTER ·

It is important to maintain a supply of water for birds during winter (p.11). Bathing is always followed by preening. Preening maintains the insulating proper-ties of the plumage, which are vital for the survival of birds in cold weather, by keeping the feathers oiled and in tip-top condition. To guarantee birds access to water keep the bath clear of ice. A bath just off the ground, such as the upturned dustbin lid, may be kept ice-free by placing a slow-burning nightlight candle underneath it. You can rush out with kettles of boiling water to melt ice as it forms but it is easier to install an aquar-ium heater and thermostat, under a pile of gravel. If you expect prolonged, severe frosts, fit two heaters. All outdoor wiring must, of course, be waterproof. If you are in any doubt consult an electrician. Never use anti-freeze or salt to stop water freezing, as these will harm the birds.

· PONDS ·

An attractive alternative to a bird-bath is a pond. There are plenty of books that give technical information on the construction and stocking of garden ponds. These details are not relevant here – suffice it to say that the simplest way to install a pond is to buy a specially moulded fibre-glass container and the cheapest is to line a hole with thick polythene sheeting. In either case, the main problem is likely to be the disposal of the excavated soil! Whatever method you choose, the pond must be suitable for a bird to use. The edges should shelve away gently so that the bird can wade in up to its middle.

Kidney-shaped pond Small birds can stand on the pile of stones to reach the water.

A platform built from either bricks or stones, or a boggy shore, planted with marsh plants (like flag irises, bogbeans and marsh marigolds), provides an area of shallower water for small birds. Blackbirds and thrushes also appreciate the water-logged soil when building their nests.

∴ NEST-BOXES ∴

Making your own nest-box is great fun. You do not need any carpentry skills – birds cannot afford to be fussy about their housing standards. Select a nest-box that suits the birds living nearby. Do not make it too small: the box should have a minimum floor size of 100 cm² (16 in²) or the nestlings may become cramped and overheat on hot days. The best wood to use is either 15 cm (6 in) floorboard, 15 mm ($^5/_8$ in) thick, or a sheet of 15 mm ($^5/_8$ in) plywood, which should be treated with a harmless preservative. (Modify the dimensions according to the thickness of the timber you use.) To stop rain entering the box, seal the joints with glue or mastic, but as this may not make the box fully waterproof, drill drainage holes in the floor. Follow either metric or imperial measurements: do not mix the two.

· STANDARD BOXES ·

Front view

Enclosed nest-box Small holes, such as the cavities found in old trees, are often in short supply in the garden. An enclosed box is a good substitute and blue and great tits usually visit a box within days of it being put up. Tack on a strip of waterproof material (inner tube or webbing is ideal) to hinge the lid, or if you do not intend to inspect the nest, simply screw the top down. To make a home exclusively for tits (a tit-box), make the entrance no more than 29 mm ($1^1/_8$ in) in diameter; otherwise, house sparrows and starlings may take over. Fix a metal plate around the hole to stop woodpeckers or squirrels enlarging it. Do not disturb the box until the fledglings have left; then open it and clean it out thoroughly. A soggy nest left inside harbours parasites and makes the box rot.

Entrance hole Make the hole using an adjustable bit, or mark out the circle and then drill a series of holes around the inside of it, joining them up afterwards with a fret-saw.

Side view
Secure the lid of the nest-box with a rust-proof hook and eye on each side. This allows you to clean out the box in autumn. It is best not to fit a perch as it encourages predators.

Front view

Open-fronted nest-box This box is a variation of the enclosed nest-box. It is used chiefly by robins and wrens, and, if much larger, occasionally kestrels. Instead of drilling an entrance hole, cut a panel to cover half the front of the box.

Preparation Both standard boxes are made in the same way. You need 1.8 m (6 ft) of 150 mm (6 in) floorboard, 15 mm (⁵/₈ in) thick, or the equivalent amount of plywood. Make full-sized paper templates of the pieces using the measurements shown below. Arrange the templates on the wood before cutting out the pieces. The side edge of the lid that butts on to the back of the box (and the top edge of the front of the enclosed box) should be sawn at an angle so the lid fits tightly.

Log box *A natural-looking box can be made from a log. Halve the log and hollow it out, drilling a hole in one of the halves. To create the nesting chamber, simply nail the halves together. Add a piece for the roof.*

Metal plate

265 mm (10¹/₂ in)

Attachment hole

150 mm (6 in)

312 mm (12¹/₄ in)

265 mm (10¹/₂ in)

Open front

Side   **Front with hole**   **Side**

Nails
38 mm (1¹/₂ in)

Hooks and eyes

Hinge   Tacks

120 mm (4³/₄ in)

Base

500 mm (20 in)

Assembly Drill a small hole at the top and bottom of the back. With 38 mm (1¹/₂ in) nails, fix the sides of the box to the base, then attach the back and front. Finally nail the lid, or use 12 mm (¹/₂ in) tacks if it is hinged.

206 mm (8 in)

Back   **Lid**

· TREECREEPER BOX ·

Front view

Treecreepers are not hole-nesters but they sometimes use specialized nest-boxes with side entrances. They will nest under a strip of curved bark, wired lengthways to a tree trunk, but you can build a more elaborate box. You will need a 1.4 m (5 ft) length of floorboard, 15 mm (⁵⁄₈ in) thick, or a comparable amount of plywood. First make a paper template for all the pieces using the measurements shown below. Lay out the templates on the wood, ensuring that the two wedge-shaped pieces are arranged to make an oblong shape. Cut the pieces out and then, to ensure the lid is flush, saw the top edge of the front piece and the back edge of the lid at an angle. To make the entrances to the box cut away the top back corners of the sides as shown below.

Assembly Make attachment holes in the back piece. Nail the sides on to the back with 38 mm (1¹⁄₂ in) ovals. Next, slide in the front and secure it in place. Finally, using 145 mm (5¹⁄₂ in) of piano hinge and brass screws, attach the lid and fix on the hook and eye.

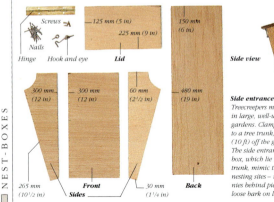

Hinge   Screws   Nails   Hook and eye

Lid 125 mm (5 in) 225 mm (9 in)

150 mm (6 in)

Side view

300 mm (12 in) 300 mm (12 in) 60 mm (2¹⁄₂ in)

480 mm (19 in)

265 mm (10¹⁄₂ in)   **Front**   **Sides**   30 mm (1¹⁄₄ in)   **Back**

Side entrance
Treecreepers may nest in large, well-wooded gardens. Clamp the box to a tree trunk, 3 m (10 ft) off the ground. The side entrances to the box, which lie next to the trunk, mimic the natural nesting sites – in crannies behind pieces of loose bark on large trees.

· TAWNY OWL BOX ·

Side view

The tawny owl does not build a nest and usually lays its eggs in an old tree hole or squirrel's drey. You can tempt a tawny owl to nest in your garden by building this specially designed, chimney-type nest-box or an open-fronted box (p.27) of the same dimensions. (Both types of nest-box may also attract jackdaws.) Cut the base and two sides from a 1.75 m (6 ft) length of 225 x 20 mm (9 x ¾ in) timber, and the other two pieces (roof and front) from a 550 x 915 mm (2 x 3 ft) sheet of ply, 12 mm (½ in) thick.

Box placement
Nail the batten to the side of a main branch of a tree so that the box lies at an angle of more than 45° to the horizontal. The projecting roof helps to keep the box dry.

Nest lining *Spread a thick layer of sawdust or peat over the bottom of the box to absorb the foulings of the nestlings.*

Assembly Drill small drainage holes in the base. Using 52 mm (2 in) nails, attach the two thick sides to the base. To complete the box, nail on the front panel and roof.

Fixing the batten
Cut a batten, 700 mm (27½ in) long and 70 mm (2¾ in) wide, and drill with holes so that it can be fixed to the box and nailed to the tree. With a bradawl, make pilot holes in the side of the box for screws (as shown in the main photograph).

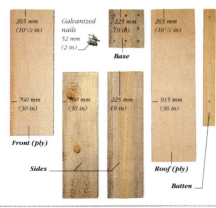

265 mm (10½ in)

Galvanized nails 52 mm (2 in)

225 mm (9 in)

Base

265 mm (10½ in)

760 mm (30 in)

760 mm (30 in)

225 mm (9 in)

915 mm (36 in)

Front (ply)

Sides

Roof (ply)

Batten

• BIRD-SHELF •

The bird-shelf, which is similar to the open-fronted box (p.27), provides a firm foundation for the nests of spotted fly-catchers, pied wagtails and blackbirds. It is cheap and easy to make and, as the size and shape are not critical, it can be made from scraps of timber. The shelf in the photograph is made from a sheet of plywood, 125 x 770 mm (5 x 30½ in) and 15 mm (⅝ in) thick. Cut out the pieces according to the measurements given.

Front view *The shelf is popular with spotted flycatchers, which like to be able to see out.*

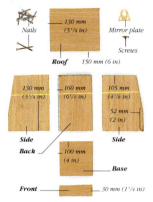

Assembly Use long nails to fix the front and back to the base, and 38 mm (1½ in) ovals for the sides. Attach the roof so that it overhangs at the front. Finally, screw on the mirror plate.

• BOWL-NEST •

House martins build deep cup-shaped nests of mud below a gutter or an eave. They usually nest in colonies at trad-itional sites but you can encourage the birds to adopt a new house by putting up artificial nests. Construct each nest from plaster-of-Paris or quick-drying cement using a 125 mm (5 in) beach ball as a mould. Chalk the outline of the nest on the ball, marking out an entrance hole 60 mm (2½ in) across and 25 mm (1 in) deep. Mould the wet material over the ball to a thickness of 9 mm (⅜ in) and embed a bracket in each side. Next, build a frame from two wooden boards, pro-tected with paint and fixed at right angles. When the bowl-nest is dry, screw it to the frame using the brackets.

Front view *Swallows may also use this man-made nest, sited inside a shed.*

Moulding the nest *Smooth the material with an old, flat knife as it dries. When it is dry, file the edges to fit the frame neatly.*

Bracket *Set brass, right-angled brackets into the material.*

ENCLOSED NEST-BOXES

	Floor size	Depth (up to entrance)	Diameter (of entrance hole)	Comments
House sparrow	15 x 15 cm (6 x 6 in)	15 cm (6 in)	32 mm ($1\frac{1}{4}$ in)	Easily disturbed
Jackdaw	20 x 20 cm ($7\frac{7}{8}$ x $7\frac{7}{8}$ in)	40 cm ($15\frac{3}{4}$ in)	150 mm (6 in)	Place in a high, secluded position.
Little owl	120 cm x 20 cm (4 ft x $7\frac{7}{8}$ in)	30 cm (12 in)	100 mm (4 in)	Partition the box to darken the hole.
Mallard	30 x 30 cm (12 x 12 in)	20 cm ($7\frac{7}{8}$ in)	150 mm (6 in)	Position on a raft or island.
Nuthatch	15 x 15 cm (6 x 6 in)	12 cm ($4\frac{3}{4}$ in)	32 mm ($1\frac{1}{4}$ in)	
Starling	15 x 15 cm (6 x 6 in)	30 cm (12 in)	52 mm (2 in)	
Street pigeon	20 x 20 cm ($7\frac{7}{8}$ x $7\frac{7}{8}$ in)	10 cm (4 in)	100 mm (4 in)	Add a perch.
Tits	15 x 12 cm (6 x $4\frac{3}{4}$ in)	12 cm ($4\frac{3}{4}$ in)	29 mm ($1\frac{1}{8}$ in)	Great tits also use larger boxes.
Woodpeckers	15 x 15 cm (6 x 6 in)	40 cm ($15\frac{3}{4}$ in)	60 mm ($2\frac{1}{2}$ in)	Place high on a trunk.

OPEN-FRONTED NEST-BOXES

	Floor size	Depth (of box)	Height (to top of front)	Comments
Kestrel	30 x 50 cm (12 x 20 in)	30 cm (12 in)	150 mm (6 in)	Fix on a 5 m (16 ft) pole. Add a perch.
Robin	10 x 10 cm (4 x 4 in)	15 cm (6 in)	52 mm (2 in)	
Wren	10 x 10 cm (4 x 4 in)	15 cm (6 in)	100 mm (4 in)	

BIRD-SHELVES

Blackbird	20 x 20 cm ($7\frac{7}{8}$ x $7\frac{7}{8}$ in)	20 cm ($7\frac{7}{8}$ in)	25 mm (1 in)	
Pied wagtail	10 x 10 cm (4 x 4 in)	10 cm (4 in)	25 mm (1 in)	Place in thick cover.
Spotted flycatcher	15 x 15 cm (6 x 6 in)	10 cm (4 in)	25 mm (1 in)	Place with a clear outlook and a perch nearby.

SPECIAL NEST-BOXES

House martin	An artificial bowl-nest (p.30)	Fasten under eaves.
Swallow	A bowl-nest (p.30), or half-coconut shell	Site inside shed.
Swift	An oblong-shaped box, 50 x 20 x 10 cm (20 x $7\frac{7}{8}$ x 4 in), with an entrance underneath.	Place horizontally beneath eaves.
Tawny owl	A chimney-type box (p.29)	Place under a branch.
Treecreeper	A wedge-shaped box, with a side entrance (p.28)	Mount against a trunk

CHAPTER TWO

BIRD PROFILES

BIRDS CAN BE enjoyed simply for their colour, movement or song, but anyone with a degree of curiosity wants to know which birds are visiting their garden. The directory of bird profiles is a superb means of identifying most of the common (and a few less common) species that you may spot in a garden or park, and describes their typical feeding and nesting habits. In particular, guidance is given, wherever possible, for distinguishing sexes and age groups. It makes it more interesting if you realize that the brownish blackbird being chased across the lawn, for example, is a young male rather than a female because it explains the intent of the glossy, black adult male that is giving chase.

A young treecreeper camouflaged against a tree

∙: WHAT BIRD IS THAT? :∙

THE PURPOSE OF *Bird Profiles* is to introduce a representative selection of common birds and describe their habits so that they become familiar figures in the garden. This reference guide will be of most help to those readers with little experience of birdwatching but who want to play host to birds in their garden and are keen to put names to faces. If you know what to look for, you are bound to have success in identifying birds.

· POSITIVE IDENTIFICATION ·

There are two possible ways to identify an unknown bird. You can either thumb through a bird book until you find the picture of a likely candidate or you can ask a knowledgable birdwatcher. Both ways only work if you observe the bird carefully and note the key features that will confirm its identity. Otherwise, the book will present a bewildering kaleido-scope of birds, which look almost, but not quite, like the one you saw. And the bird-watcher will not be able to match your vague description with the pictures in his mental field guide. Make notes of a bird's size and obvious physical features but

also record details, such as voice, flight pattern, posture at rest, how the bird walks and where it was seen.

I was once stumped by a request to name a "black and white" bird. I worked through magpie, pied wagtail, long-tailed tit and spotted woodpecker – but none was right. Finally the puzzle was solved by the clue that the bird was seen flying away from fruit bushes. What was glimpsed was a bullfinch! – from behind, its black cap, back and tail contrasted with its white rump. Once realized, it was obvious, but I would have got there quicker if I had been given its rough size.

THE PARTS OF A BIRD'S BODY

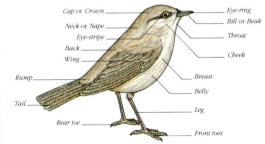

Cap or *Crown*
Neck or *Nape*
Eye-stripe
Back
Wing
Rump
Tail
Rear toe
Eye-ring
Bill or *Beak*
Throat
Cheek
Breast
Belly
Leg
Front toes

Recording the details Use the names above when taking notes. Trace over the drawing so you have an outline that you can quickly fill in with details of your mystery bird. Register its colours and the size, shape and colour of the

bill and legs. Look carefully at any stripe on the face: does it run through the eye or above it? It is important to judge the bird's size: com-pare it with known birds, such as sparrows or starlings, or else a leaf or a brick in a wall.

· THE BIRD PROFILE ·

Forty-five bird species are listed here within their family groups, according to the conventional order of scientific classification. Both the common and scientific names of the family and species are given. Any significant features of each bird are described in detail for ease of identification. The information provided on feeding and nesting will help you meet the needs of particular birds.

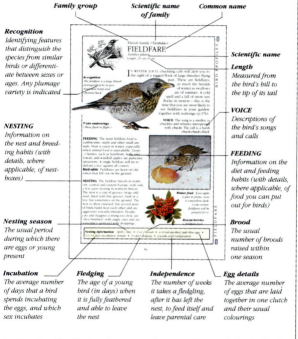

Family group

Scientific name of family

Common name

Recognition
Identifying features that distinguish the species from similar birds or differentiate between sexes or ages. Any plumage variety is indicated

NESTING
Information on the nest and breeding habits (with details, where applicable, of nest-boxes)

Nesting season
The usual period during which there are eggs or young present

Incubation
The average number of days that a bird spends incubating the eggs, and which sex incubates

Fledging
The age of a young bird (in days) when it is fully feathered and able to leave the nest

Independence
The number of weeks it takes a fledgling, after it has left the nest, to feed itself and leave parental care

Scientific name

Length
Measured from the bird's bill to the tip of its tail

VOICE
Descriptions of the bird's songs and calls

FEEDING
Information on the diet and feeding habits (with details, where applicable, of food you can put out for birds)

Brood
The usual number of broods raised within one season

Egg details
The average number of eggs that are laid together in one clutch and their usual colourings

Within the profile image:

Thrush family *(Turdidae)*
FIELDFARE
Turdus pilaris
Length: 25 cm (10 in)

Recognition
The fieldfare is a large thrush distinguished by its grey head and chestnut back

I N WINTER, LOUD, chuckling calls will alert you to the sight of a ragged flock of large thrushes flying past. These are fieldfares, as much the heralds of winter as swallows are of summer. A cold spell and a fall of snow sets flocks in motion – this is the time that you are most likely to see fieldfares in your garden, together with redwings (p.176).

Pale underwings
(These flash in flight.)

VOICE The song is a medley of chuckles and whistles interspersed with *chacks*. The call is a harsh *chack-chack-chack.*

FEEDING The main fieldfare food is earthworms, snails and other small animals. Fruit is eaten in winter, especially when animal food is unavailable. Crops of berries, such as hawthorn, holly and rowan, and windfall apples are particular attractions. A single fieldfare will try to defend a tree against all comers.
Bird-table: Fieldfares are keen on old, rotten fruit left out on the ground.

NESTING The fieldfare breeds in northern, central and eastern Europe, with only a few pairs nesting in northern Britain. The nest is a cup of grasses, twigs and mud, lined with fine grasses, built in a tree but sometimes on the ground. The nest is often exposed, but several pairs of birds build near each other and are aggressive towards intruders. People, cats and magpies coming too close are dive-bombed with angry cries and are sometimes spattered with droppings.

Winter fruit *If an apple is past its prime, store it somewhere dark and a winter-visiting fieldfare will be grateful for it*

Rowan berries *Fieldfares feed on these in the autumn*

Nesting information
Nesting season	Incubation	Fledging	Independence	Brood	Egg details
April – May	13 – 14 days in situation	1 or 2 broods	14 days fledging	4–6 red-speckled, pale-blue eggs	2 weeks until independent

35

Nesting information The figures (placed in the box at the bottom of the page) for brood and egg numbers, incubation, fledging and independence times are only approximate. They are likely to vary, depending on circumstances. For example, first-time breeders tend to lay fewer eggs than the average range indicated above. The availability of food is another important factor that influences the size of a clutch of eggs.

Heron family *(Ardeidae)*

GREY HERON

Ardea cinerea
Length: 90 cm (36 in)

T HE HERON IS a wary bird that rarely comes into the garden but steals fish or frogs from ponds when it does. Once a heron has found the source of an easy meal, it is likely to return until it has cleaned out the pond. Unless you make a special point of keeping watch when it sneaks in at dawn or dusk, you will spot one only if it is disturbed, as it rises steeply to make a hurried escape.

Black plumes

Dagger-like bill

Recognition
The heron is a very large bird with long legs and neck.

Grey plumage above

FEEDING The heron mainly eats fish, amphibians and large insects, but also small mammals and other animals.
Bird-table Assorted meat scraps are sometimes taken in hard weather.

White underneath

Flight *The grey heron flies on broad wings with head held in and legs trailing.*

Pond robber *A heron swallows a goldfish.*

VOICE The most common call that you are likely to hear is a harsh *fraank*.

NESTING The heron nests in tall trees (rarely on buildings), usually alongside several other nests in a *beronry*, which may be hundreds of years old. The nest, which consists of a large platform of twigs, is built by both sexes and lined with grass. The heronry is often used as a communal winter roost. Breeding starts early in the year, with most of the eggs being laid by early April.

Nesting information February – July • 1 brood • 4 or 5 pale blue eggs • 25–26 days incubation: both sexes • 50 days fledging • 2–3 weeks until independent

Duck family *(Anatidae)*

MALLARD

Anas platyrhynchos
Length: 58 cm (23 in)

Recognition *A white ring separates the drake's (male's) bottle-green head from his breast.*

Plumage After the male has accompanied the female to the nest, he moults into the *eclipse* plumage, similar to the female's brown, mottled plumage *(below)*. Ducks shed all their flight-feathers at once and become flightless. After the breeding season, males moult back into their brilliant colouring.

PROBABLY ONE OF the best-known birds, the mallard is the ancestor of almost all domestic ducks. It visits rural gardens where there is a pond, or if the garden is near a lake or river. Mallards may nest in large gardens that have plenty of cover. The female may need your help in leading her ducklings safely across roads to water.

MALE

Wing-patch (speculum) – *bright blue or purple, edged with black and white, on both sexes*

FEMALE

VOICE There is a variety of quacks made. The female emits a harsh series of quacks, whereas the male has quieter, nasal quacks.

FEEDING Mallards eat a wide range of food; watch them grazing on lawns, eating acorns and hunting for water-snails, caddis fly larvae, frogs or fish in shallow water. Ducklings feed mainly on insects.
Bird-table Mallards take bread and grain in parks and gardens.

NESTING The nest of leaves and grasses is placed under dense vegetation, sometimes in a tree. The female, who rears the family by herself, covers the nest with down when she leaves to feed. The eggs hatch together and the ducklings depart the nest before they are a day old.
Nest-box Large enclosed box (p.31).

Insulation Eggs are kept warm by downy feathers.

Nesting information March – October • 1 brood • 8–12 grey-green eggs • 27–28 days incubation: female • 50–60 days fledging • Independent at fledging

Falcon family *(Falconidae)*

KESTREL
Falco tinnunculus
Length: 34 cm (13¹/₂ in)

Grey head

Male *The adult male has a grey head and tail. (The female has a barred black and brown tail.)*

Pointed wings

Streaked breast

Mouse

I N RECENT YEARS the kestrel was the bird of prey most often seen around gardens until the sparrowhawk population recovered from widespread pesticide poisoning. The kestrel is the easier bird to recognize because of its habit of floating in a stiff breeze or hovering in the air with rapidly whirring wings. Although strenuous, hovering allows the kestrel to cover wide areas when scanning for prey on the ground.

Recognition *The kestrel can be distinguished from the sparrowhawk by its more pointed wings and streaked breast.*

VOICE During the breeding season, listen for a shrill *kee-kee-kee*.

FEEDING The main prey is rodents, large insects and earthworms, but kestrels may ambush small birds by dashing behind hedges, like a sparrowhawk.
Bird-table Meat scraps, and even fat and biscuits, are taken on rare occasions.

Remains *Bones of rodents are regurgitated in a pellet.*

NESTING No nest is built but a lining of sticks and straw may be added to a hole in a tree, an old nest or a ledge on cliffs and buildings.
Nest-box Open-fronted nest-box (p.31).

Bird of prey *A juvenile kestrel tears beakfuls of flesh from a mouse.*

Nesting information *April – July • 1 brood • 4 or 5 brown-blotched, white eggs • 27–29 days incubation: female • 27–32 days fledging • 4 weeks until independent*

Pheasant family *(Phasianidae)*

PHEASANT

Phasianus colchicus
Length: Male 84 cm (33 in); Female 58 cm (23 in)

Dark green head
Red face

Recognition *Whether magnificently copper-coloured like this male or drab brown like the female (below right), a pheasant cannot be confused with any other bird in the garden.*

THE ROMANS CARRIED the pheasant through Europe from Asia and it was introduced to Britain by the Normans. It enters gardens usually in autumn and winter, especially in hard weather. You are more likely to see cock pheasants because the females keep to the woods. As with other birds in which the male is colourful and the female dull, the female is wholly responsible for raising the family.

MALE

Foraging
A male pecks at the ground for grain. Some individuals have a white neck-ring.

VOICE
The male's song is a loud *kork-kok*, which the female replies to with a *kea, kea*. There is a *kut-ok, kut-ok* of alarm. The female has a variety of calls that causes her brood to hide.

FEEDING Pheasants scratch for a wide range of foods, especially grain and other seeds and acorns, and clamber in trees for buds and fruit. Animal food includes insects, snails, worms and occasionally small mammals and lizards. Grass, leaves and roots are eaten in winter.
Bird-table Pheasants eat grain, bread and kitchen leftovers.

NESTING The female nests in a shallow depression, under a hedge or in long grass or bracken. The chicks leave the nest shortly after hatching.

Camouflage *A female incubating the eggs in her nest on the ground blends perfectly with the surrounding dead bracken.*

Nesting information March – July • 1 brood • 8–15 olive-brown eggs • 23–28 days incubation: female • 12 days fledging • 9–10 weeks until independent

BIRD PROFILES

PHEASANT

Rail family *(Rallidae)*

MOORHEN

Gallinula chloropus
Length: 33 cm (13 in)

THE MOORHEN IS most often seen in parks, where it stalks daintily across the grass around lakes, but a garden pond also entices and, if there is enough cover, a moorhen may nest there. Watch for moorhens in trees: they are surprisingly agile and regularly roost on branches. Young moorhens of the first brood stay with their parents and help feed their younger siblings of the second.

Red bill and shield (absent in young)

White feathers under tail

White line on flank

VOICE A loud, sharp *purruk* often gives away the moorhen's presence.

Toes *Moorhens fight fierce territorial battles with their feet and, as a result, can easily end up with broken toes.*

FEEDING The moorhen takes small animals, such as worms, snails and fish, and a variety of leaves, seeds and berries.
Bird-table Bread and fat on the ground.

Breadwinner *A moorhen (right) eats a crust.*

NESTING The nest is constructed from twigs and dead reeds among water vegetation, but also in hedges or trees, and is lined with finer plants. The male gathers most of the material while the female builds the nest. If the water level rises during incubation, more material is added to lift the eggs clear.

Chick *A two-week old moorhen finds its own food but receives extra rations from its parents.*

Nesting information *April – August • 2 or 3 broods • 5 – 8 dark-spotted, buff eggs • 21 – 22 days incubation: both sexes • 40 – 50 days fledging • 1 – 7 weeks until independent*

Rail family *(Rallidae)*

COOT

Fulica atra

Length: 38 cm (15 in)

White shield on face (missing when young)

Compared with its relative, the moorhen, the coot is a more aquatic species that prefers larger ponds and lakes, even slow-flowing rivers. This makes it less likely to come into gardens but it is common in parks and on urban reservoirs. Watch for conflicts between rivals, in which one coot races after another over the water or fights by sitting back on its tail and kicking and clawing. Sometimes a flock unites to drive away a gull or hawk by kicking up a shower of water.

VOICE A loud *kowk* is the most common of a number of calls.

Fishing A coot eats a stickleback. Before diving, coots squeeze air from their plumage to decrease their buoyancy.

Fleshy lobes on toes – a swimming aid

Great ramshorn snail shell

FEEDING Water plants, fish and animals, such as snails, beetles and bugs, are brought up from the bottom of ponds, or stolen from swans and ducks. Small mammals and birds may be taken on land.

Bird-table Although rare garden feeders, coots eat scraps, bread and grain.

Pond food The coot eats a broad variety of small animals and plant food found in water.

Fool's watercress *Hornwort*

NESTING The nest is a pile of vegetation built in shallow water. The male collects most of the material, which the female works into place. After the eggs hatch, the male builds a platform where he roosts and broods the young at night.

Tending the young Both parents feed the young for about eight weeks.

Nesting information March – September • 1 or 2 broods • 4–7 speckled, buff eggs •
21–24 days incubation: both sexes • 55–60 days fledging • Independent at fledging

Gull family *(Laridae)*

BLACK-HEADED GULL

Larus ridibundus
Length: 38 cm (15 in)

Aᴌᴛʜᴏᴜɢʜ ʙᴀꜱɪᴄᴀʟʟʏ a seabird, the black-headed gull has moved inland this century, replacing the crow and kite as the urban scavenger. At first, black-headed gulls were winter visitors to towns and returned to the coast to breed. The species started to nest near to towns some time afterwards but inland breeding colonies have remained small. The inland gull roosts and nests in gravel pits, reservoirs and sewage works and commutes daily to feed on farmland and in city parks and gardens.

Dark spot on head

VOICE
There is a variety of harsh calls, including a repeated *kek* of alarm.

Winter plumage
After the nesting season, the dark brown head-feathers disappear, except for marks behind the eyes.

Young gull
Juveniles are a mottled, pale brown. By the time they are a year old, they have orange legs and beak, but retain some brown on the wings.

Red legs

FEEDING Black-headed gulls mainly eat insects and worms seized from the ground or stolen from other birds. They circle in upcurrents to catch flying ants and scavenge around dumps and waste ground.
Bird-table Gulls swoop down for scraps.

NESTING Black-headed gulls breed in colonies with nests close together. The simple nest of grass is built on the ground or, very exceptionally, on buildings.

Black head *A gull in summer breeding-dress carries food in its bulging crop (neck pouch).*

Nesting information *April – July • 1 brood • 3 brown-blotched, grey-green eggs • 23–26 days incubation: both sexes • 35 days fledging • 1 week until independent*

Pigeon family *(Columbidae)*

COLLARED DOVE
Streptopelia decaocto
Length: 32 cm (12½ in)

Black and white collar *(lacking in the juvenile)*

VOICE A repeated *coo-COO-coo* advertises the territory and is used in courtship. Although initially a gentle, pleasing sound, the monotonous cooing may become infuriating. Sometimes, when the collared dove gives only two *coos,* you may mistake it for the cuckoo. The dove gives a nasal *whurr-whurr* when excited, as in the male's display flight, which is similar to the woodpigeon's (p.46).

A LTHOUGH A COMMON bird over much of the country, the collared dove is a relative newcomer. Sixty years ago it started to spread westwards from its native home in south-eastern Europe. This tame and attractive bird reached Britain in the 1950s, and is now found over most of Europe. Perhaps because its new home is colder, the collared dove prefers to live in towns and villages, or near farms, where it can find plenty of food.

Pale grey and brown plumage

Elder *The purple berries are often eaten by collared doves.*

FEEDING The collared dove mainly eats seeds with some leaves, buds and fruit but occasionally feeds on caterpillars, snails and other small animals.
Bird-table It frequently feeds on grain, seeds, bread and scraps.

NESTING The female builds a flimsy platform of twigs in a tree, occasionally on a building, while the male gathers material. The nestlings are fed on *pigeon's milk* (p.47). Parents drive jays, magpies and even humans away from the nest.

Squabs – collared dove nestlings

Nesting information *March – November* • *3–6 broods* • *2 white eggs* • *14–18 days incubation: both sexes (female at night)* • *17 days fledging* • *1 week until independent*

Pigeon family *(Columbidae)*

STREET PIGEON

Columba livia

Length: 33 cm (13 in)

Neck-patch
The glossy lilac and green is typical of the rock dove.

T HIS FAMILIAR INHABITANT of towns and cities is a descendant of the rock dove that, centuries ago, was domesticated and selectively bred in dovecotes. The rock dove was kept for the table, for carrying messages or for racing in competitions. Street (or feral) pigeons are the wild descendants of a variety of domestic breeds and their numbers are continually being increased by domestic pigeons, still bred for show and racing, that have escaped from captivity or become lost on homing flights.

Plumage
Pigeons are usually grey-blue, marked with white – often on the rump.

Sunbathing *A domestic pigeon basks on the warm ground during summer sunshine. Although the street pigeon population is self-supporting, numbers are increased by a variety of breeds of domestic pigeon returning to the wild.*

VOICE The low, cooing *ooor-ooor* or *o-roo-coo* is a familiar sound in cities.

Living on the streets Street pigeons make friends by becoming hand-tame in parks and squares, but they are a problem for municipal authorities because they foul buildings and may spread disease. Despite attempts by authorities to restrict numbers, the bonanza of easily procured food in towns lets the pigeon population build up and allows many sick and injured pigeons to survive much longer than they would in natural conditions. As a result, you often see street pigeons with deformed legs or damaged bills.

Grounded *A racing pigeon takes its bearings before flying to its home loft. Racing breeds have a remarkable homing ability; competitors enter them in races of up to 500 miles long.*

44

BIRD PROFILES

Flight *Strong breast-muscles and a heavy body make pigeons powerful fliers.*

FEEDING Street pigeons eat any spilt grain, seeds, bread and other edible litter. At one time grain from horses' nosebags was an important food but nowadays litter from fast-food outlets provides a ready supply. Many urban pigeons take at least some of their food from handouts in squares and parks. Some pigeons even learn to recognize individuals who provide food regularly and will approach these people when they appear.
Bird-table Grain, bread and kitchen scraps.

Cultivated grain

Fan-shaped tail *The garden fantail, seen feeding on seeds under the bird-table, is a variety of pigeon that breeds well in dovecotes.*

NESTING The nest of twigs is built by the female, with the assistance of the male, on a ledge or in a hole. Pairs may nest all year if conditions are favourable. As with other members of the pigeon family, nestlings are only given solid food after a period of 10 days (p.47).
Nest–box Enclosed nest-box (p.31). Dovecotes – wooden "houses" separated into compartments – are also used, both for roosting and nesting.

Brooding A street pigeon settles down on the nest and covers a squab (a young pigeon) to protect it and keep it warm.

STREET PIGEON

Nesting information Mainly March – September • 2 or 3 broods • 2 white eggs •
17–18 days incubation: both sexes • 49 days fledging • 1 week until independent

Pigeon family *(Columbidae)*

WOODPIGEON

Columba palumbus
Length: 40 cm (16 in)

White and green neck-patch
(The juvenile lacks this patch and is duller overall.)

I N THE COUNTRYSIDE, farmers regard the woodpigeon as a pest because of its appetite for cereals, root crops and legumes. Normally wary as a result, this large pigeon becomes tame in built-up areas, where you may see it walking towards a supply of food or water with a typically "pigeon-toed" gait. The male often advertises his presence in the territory, which may be no more than a single tree, simply by sitting conspicuously: a woodpigeon in a bare tree is difficult to miss.

Wing-flash *A striking, white wing-flash separates the black outer wing and grey inner wing – most noticeable when in flight.*

VOICE The song is a plaintive c*oo* COO c*oo* c*oo-coo*, the first faint note of which is easily missed. A bout of cooing ends with a final c*ook*. You may hear a softer cooing during courtship, when the male bows before the female with his plumage puffed out and tail fanned.

Take-off When flying off, the woodpigeon's wings meet over its back with a sharp clap. The man-oeuvre is so strenuous that it will not be repeated in a hurry. Once disturbed, the bird settles in a tree, from which it can effortlessly launch itself by dropping.

Wing-claps

Glide

Display flight You will see the display flight, which is a steep climb and glide, mostly in February and March (some time after the males take up territories in winter). At the top of the arc, one or two loud wing-claps can be heard. These are whipcracks on the down-stroke rather than the wings striking together.

Black-tipped tail

46

Beak The slightly hooked beak – not found on other European pigeons – is designed for tearing leaves.

FEEDING The woodpigeon likes legumes, especially peas and beans, and brassicas, such as cabbages, swedes, turnips and brussels sprouts. Other foods are acorns, beech mast, haws, elders and weed seeds, as well as worms, snails and insects. Do not be surprised to see a pigeon eating grit – it is used to grind food in its *gizzard* (the muscular part of the stomach).
Bird-table A rare visitor, the woodpigeon may come to ground stations for bread, seeds and vegetable scraps. It is more likely to visit for a drink at a garden pond or bird-bath.

Ivy food In winter, look for woodpigeons eating ivy berries.

Beech mast – a favoured food

Beak used as drinking-straw

Simple bird-bath (p.109)

Unique drinking Pigeons put their beaks into water and suck; other birds raise their heads to let water trickle down their throats.

Garden pest Woodpigeons do serious damage to sprouts and cabbages in winter.

NESTING Both parents assemble a flimsy platform, usually in a tree but sometimes on a building, from twigs gathered from the ground or snapped off trees. Eggs (laid at one- to three-day intervals) can be seen on the floor of the nest. If the nest is re-used, it becomes bulkier. The long nesting season is a result of the woodpigeon's ability to feed its *squabs* (nestlings) on *pigeon's milk* – a cheesy secretion from the crop, rich in protein and fat. Most other garden birds feed their young on insects, which are only available over a limited season.

Nesting information February – November • 2 broods • 2 white eggs • 17 days incubation: both sexes • 20–35 days fledging • 1 week until independent

WOODPIGEON

Owl family *(Strigidae)*

TAWNY OWL

Strix aluco
Length: 38 cm (15 in)

MORE OFTEN HEARD than seen because of its nocturnal lifestyle, the tawny owl is the most common hunting bird in gardens, preying mainly on small mammals (such as moles) and birds but also catching fish, amphibians, reptiles, worms, beetles and moths. Although it is rare to see a tawny owl by day, do keep a watch as it likes to sunbathe from time to time. Essentially a bird of mature woodlands, the tawny owl has been able to adapt even to city life where there are enough large trees, which are needed for roosting-places as well as nest sites.

VOICE The song is a hollow *hooo* followed by a wavering *hoo-hoo-hoo-ooooo*. A sharp *ke-wick* call is used by a pair to keep in contact. Listen for young owls repeatedly calling with a hissing *ke-sip* throughout summer nights.

Behaviour When alarmed, the tawny owl makes its body as slender as possible (here, it turns its head almost full circle to keep an eye on the threat). In contrast, in an aggressive posture, the owl widens its eyes and fluffs out its feathers to make itself appear larger.

Recognition
A tawny owl, with its unmistakable silhouette, is only likely to be confused with the much smaller little owl (p.50).

Alarm posture
Body is slender.

Aggressive posture
Owl widens body.

FEEDING Tawny owls in country gardens mainly catch mice and voles but town owls, like kestrels, chiefly feed on birds, up to the size of pigeons and mallards. Garden birds are killed mostly at dawn or dusk when they are just active but tawny owls have also been seen taking birds from their roosts. They also attack nests, dragging away the sitting adult and stealing the contents. Birds are plucked first and any prey that is initially too large to swallow is carried to a perch

Ambush
*A tawny owl watches
from a perch, then
swoops down on prey.*

Silencers
*The fluffy fringes of
flight-feathers deaden
the sound of wing beats.*

and dismembered. Remains from plucking and pellets regurgitated after a meal accumulate on the ground, allowing the owl's diet to be studied. Although owls have good eyesight, prey is detected mainly by ear. Consequently rain and wind hamper hunting, although earthworms are easier to find on damp, warm nights when they come to the surface to feed and mate. The owl lands, listens intently then hops over the ground to seize the worm. Bad weather may force tawny owls to feed on carrion, such as animals killed on roads.

NESTING The tawny owl lays its eggs in a hole in a tree or building, or finds an abandoned squirrel or magpie nest. The eggs hatch at three- to four-day intervals. The young remain in the parents' territory and are fed by them until driven away when about three months old.
Nest-box Tawny owls will use a specially designed nest-box (p.29), particularly if natural sites are scarce.

Owlet *A fledgling tawny owl, with
its distinctively barred, downy
plumage, tries out its wings.*

Bird-table Tawny owls swoop down on bird-tables chiefly to catch small birds feeding there. The rare instances of tawny owls coming to feed on meat and fat are usually the result of severe weather.

Owl pellets *If you come across
dried pellets (regurgitated,
indigestible fur
and bones) on the
ground, look up and
you may discover a
tawny owl's roost.*

Nesting information March – June • 1 brood • 3 or 4 white eggs • 28–30 days
incubation: female • 32–37 days fledging • 12 weeks until independent

---

Owl family *(Strigidae)*

LITTLE OWL
Athene noctua
Length: 22 cm (8½ in)

Recognition
This small, grey-brown owl is only half the size of a tawny owl (pp.48–9).

PARKLAND WITH TREES, even in towns and cities, is a favourite habitat of the little owl, which may stray into gardens. It is more visible than the tawny owl as it often hunts by day, especially when there are nestlings to feed. You are most likely to see one when it is hunting from a perch on a tree or fence post.

VOICE The male's hoot is a plaintive *kiew-kiew*, which the female answers with a scream. The call is a *kee-oo*.

FEEDING The little owl drops from its perch to prey on earthworms and insects, such as beetles, as well as small mammals and birds, and sometimes runs after them. It also chases craneflies and other flying insects with a bound-ing flight that is unique among owls.

Meal A little owl eats an earthworm.

NESTING There is no proper nest; the eggs are laid in a hole in a tree or building, or even in a rabbit hole. The young owls, which are more uniformly grey, may leave the nest before they can fly to explore along branches or vegeta-tion. Warning calls from their parents send them scuttling back to safety.
Nest-box A large enclosed nest-box, partitioned to make it dark (p.31).

Nest site The dark hole of an oak tree is ideal.

Nesting information April – July • 1 brood • 3–5 white eggs • 27–28 days
incubation: female • 30–35 days fledging • 4 weeks until independent

Swift family *(Apodidae)*

SWIFT

Apus apus
Length: 16.5 cm (6½ in)

Slender wings

Uniformly dark plumage

N O OTHER BIRD spends as much time in the air as the swift. After nesting, it may not land again until it returns to its nest the next spring, after mating on the wing. On summer evenings, flocks gather and then circle skywards until lost to sight. They spend the night in a semi-slumber, drifting with the wind, and descend at dawn. Swifts have short legs and rarely perch, preferring to cling on to walls.

VOICE A screaming *sree*; also a chirping at the nest.

High flier *Swifts will fly up over half a mile high to catch insects, such as aphids, beetles and flying ants, carried up in turbulent air.*

Short, forked tail

FEEDING Swifts mainly feed on small flying insects and spiders floating on gossamer. They gather over lakes to feed on swarming midges. In cold, wet spells, flying insects disappear, causing swifts to travel long distances to find food.

Recognition
The swift is distinguished from the swallow and martins by its short, forked tail and long, scythe-shaped wings.

NESTING The swift's nest is a shallow cup of grasses, leaves and feathers, collected in the air and cemented with saliva. You can locate the site in holes in walls and under eaves when a bird flies up to it and then swoops away, leaving the occupants screaming. Nestlings put on weight rapidly and, by becoming torpid, can survive for a long time without being fed or brooded.

White throat

Juvenile *The fledging period depends on the availability of food.*

Nest-box Swifts will nest in a special box (p.31), with an entrance hole underneath.

Nesting information Late May–August • 1 brood • 2 or 3 white eggs • 20–22 days incubation: both sexes • 5–7 weeks fledging • Independent at fledging

Woodpecker family *(Picidae)*

GREEN WOODPECKER

Picus viridis
Length: 32 cm (12 1/2 in)

LARGE SIZE and bold colours make the green woodpecker an exciting visitor but it is not a common garden bird. Its bill, which is weaker than that of other woodpeckers, is used for chiselling soft wood only. Green woodpeckers drill holes into lawns where there are ants' nests, and push their long tongues into the soil to eat the insects.

Juvenile The juvenile is speckled and barred. (The adult has a black face, red crown and yellow rump.)

Tip of the tongue
The tongue can be extended 10 cm (4 in) so its flat, sticky tip can reach insects living deep in holes and crevices.

VOICE Loud, laughing calls can be heard.

FEEDING Woodpeckers mainly eat ants but also prey on beetles, moths and flies.
Bird-table On rare occasions, green woodpeckers take fat and mealworms.

NESTING Green woodpeckers may nest in large gardens if they can find suitable trees in which to excavate holes. The nest has a depth of up to 50 cm (20 in), and an entrance 6 cm (2 1/2 in) in diameter. It may be re-used in succeeding years, but starlings tend to take it over.
Nest-box Green woodpeckers may use large enclosed nest-boxes (p.31).

Nest hole A woodpecker takes two to three weeks to excavate its chamber. (Close-up, you can spot the male by the red in his moustache.)

Nesting information April – July • 1 brood • 5–7 white eggs • 17–19 days incubation: both sexes (male at night) • 23–27 days fledging • 3–7 weeks until independent

Woodpecker family *(Picidae)*

GREAT SPOTTED WOODPECKER

Dendrocopos major
Length: 23 cm (9 in)

Sharp bill

A MIXED BLESSING in gardens, the great spotted woodpecker is an interesting visitor but it raids nest-boxes to eat young birds inside. Like other woodpeckers, the great spotted woodpecker has a stiff tail and unusual arrangement of toes – two face forwards and two backwards. These help it climb up trees and provide a firm base when the bird chisels wood to excavate holes.

Recognition *It is larger than the lesser spotted woodpecker and has white patches on its short wings and red under its tail. The male has a crimson nape.*

VOICE The "song" is a rapid (20 times per second) drumming of the bill on a branch, which sounds like a snore (the note varies according to the size and type of branch). A loud *chick* is used as a contact call.

Drilling *Holes are bored in tree trunks to extract insects.*

FEEDING A variety of insects is eaten, from wood-boring beetles to flies caught in the air. Vegetable food includes pine, larch and spruce seeds, the seeds of birch and other hardwood trees as well as nuts, fruit and fungi. In Europe, but rarely in Britain, this woodpecker punctures trunks to drink sap.

Bird-table Suet, oats or nuts, in a birdfeeder or wedged in crevices.

Almonds – opened by woodpeckers

NESTING Both sexes excavate the nest chamber, usually 3–5 m (10–16 ft) above ground. The hole, which is about 30 cm (12 in) deep, 12 cm (4¾ in) in diameter and has an entrance of 6 cm (2½ in) wide, takes up to four weeks to complete. The same hole is used in successive years, unless it is usurped by starlings.

Nest-box Great spotted woodpeckers may use large enclosed boxes (p.31).

Nesting information April – July • 1 brood • 4–7 white eggs • 10–13 days incubation: both sexes (male at night) • 21 days fledging • 1 week until independent

Swallow family *(Hirundinidae)*

HOUSE MARTIN
Delichon urbica
Length: 12.5 cm (5 in)

VOICE There is a soft, twittering song and chirping contact notes between mates, and between parents and offspring.

Blue-black above

White underneath

Steep climb
– to snap up insects

I**N THE DAYS** before buildings provided support for its nests, the house martin occupied cliffs and rock outcrops, where colonies can still be seen. Nowadays it often builds under the eaves or on a window frame of a house. The householder who is tired of cleaning soiled windows should fix a "splashboard" over the window.

Recognition
The house martin has shorter tail-streamers than a swallow. The white rump is conspicuous in flight.

FEEDING House martins feed on flying insects, mainly flies and aphids, but they may pick prey from the ground. Typically, a house martin suddenly climbs steeply, snaps an insect, then glides down.

NESTING Soon after house martins have returned in spring they prospect for suitable nest sites. The cup-nest is built with pellets of mud from the edge of puddles or ponds and is lined with feathers and grasses collected in the air. When the nestlings are grown, you can see their heads appear at the entrance. Adults try to lure them from the nest by hovering in front of it and calling. Eventually an adult bird lands at the nest, the youngster emerges and flies away with it. Later, you can see the fledglings meeting their parents in the air to receive food.
Nest-box Place bowl-nests (p.30) underneath the eaves for house martins.

Invitation to fly An adult house martin, which is not necessarily a parent, beckons to the nestlings as it flies past, tempting them to leave the safety of the nest for the first time.

Nesting information Late May – September • 1 or 2 broods • 2–5 white eggs • 15 days incubation: both sexes • 22–32 days fledging • Time until independent unknown

---

Swallow family *(Hirundinidae)*

SWALLOW
Hirundo rustica
Length: 19 cm (7¹/₂ in)

W HEN THE SWALLOW, the traditional herald of spring, arrives, you are most likely to see it over lakes and reservoirs, where there is an abundant supply of early insects. Occasionally there are reports of swallows remaining behind to winter in Europe rather than migrating back to Africa.

Distinctive russet throat and forebead

FEMALE

VOICE The song is a pleasant, rather quiet twittering. The contact call is a repeated *swit-swit-swit.*

Recognition
Long tail-streamers and more pointed wings distinguish the adult swallow from its close relatives, the sand and house martins.

FEEDING The swallow forages for insects in the air, either swooping low or circling overhead in graceful movements that are punctuated by swift, jinking turns. The long tail-feathers provide great flight manoeuvrability, making the swallow more efficient at catching prey than swifts

or martins. If flying insects are scarce, the swallow may take insects from leaves or the ground. Bluebottle-sized flies are preferred but butterflies, moths and other large insects are also caught. Greenfly and other tiny insects are hunted by swallows in cold weather.

NESTING The beams and ledges of buildings have almost replaced cliff-side ledges as sites for the saucer of mud and grass. (During a dry spell in the garden, water a patch of soil to provide mud.) The male circles above his chosen site, singing to attract a female. Sometimes eggs are laid in a neighbour's nest.
Nest-box Make a bowl-nest (p.30).

Feeding the young The nestlings are fed with balls of insects from their parents' throats.

Nesting information May – August • 2 or 3 broods • 4 or 5 red-spotted, white eggs • 14 – 15 days incubation: female • 19 – 21 days fledging • Several weeks until independent

Pipit family *(Motacillidae)*

PIED WAGTAIL

Motacilla alba
Length: 18 cm (7 in)

Aᴌᴛʜᴏᴜɢʜ ᴇssᴇɴᴛɪᴀʟʟʏ a waterside bird, the pied wagtail has adapted to man-made habitats. You can see it feeding in gardens, parks, on top of houses or picking its way over rubbish tips. The best time for watching wagtails is when they come on to lawns to gather small insects for their offspring. The long tail gives the wagtail superb manoeuvrability as it runs across the grass to lunge at prey or springs up to snap winged insects.

Recognition *Wagtails have bold black and white plumage, but in winter, the black throat turns white.*

Tail *When standing still, wagtails continually bob their long tails. Why they do this is a mystery.*

VOICE The pied wagtail gives a loud, sharp *chissick* in flight and also sounds a musical *chee-wee* in defence of territory.

FEEDING Pied wagtails feed on small insects, especially flies, and other animals, such as small snails and earthworms, and they occasionally eat small seeds.
Bird-table Stale crumbs are taken from the ground, especially in hard weather.

Hunt *Look out for a pied wagtail (right) scurrying across the lawn when hunting.*

NESTING The cup-nest of grass, roots and mosses is built in a hole in walls, buildings, piles of brushwood or old nests of larger birds. You may identify a female as her tail becomes bent from incubating.
Nest-box Place a bird-shelf (p.30) among ivy or other thick vegetation.

Out of the nest *A parent feeds a fledgling. The juvenile's tail is much shorter.*

Nesting information *April – August • 2 broods • 3–5 brown-freckled, whitish eggs • 13 days incubation: mainly female • 14 days fledging • 1 week until independent*

Wren family *(Troglodytidae)*

WREN

Troglodytes troglodytes
Length: 9.5 cm (3¾ in)

T HE ONLY EUROPEAN member of its family, the tiny, reddish-brown wren often appears mouse-like as it scurries along the edges of walls and borders and through undergrowth. Because the wren feeds on the ground, its food is cut off by ice and snow, and the population drops in a bad winter. Put up "umbrellas" of cut conifer branches to provide snow-free patches if there are no shrubs or hedges.

Forceps-like beak

VOICE A loud, shrill trilling is sung all year round, except in late summer and early autumn. Calls include a hard *tick-tick-tick* and a rolling *churr.*

Tell-tale   Look for the characteristic short, cocked tail.

FEEDING As well as tiny aphids plucked off leaves with their forceps-like beaks, wrens snatch caterpillars, grubs and spiders. Amazingly, wrens have been known to steal small goldfish from ponds.

NESTING The male constructs several nests in holes in walls, banks and trees or in old nests of other birds. The nest is a globe of dead leaves, grass and moss with a side entrance. The male sings near a nest to entice a female to it. If she accepts, she adds a lining of feathers and lays the eggs. When food is abundant, a male may persuade two or more females to lay in his territory.

Nest-box Wrens nest in open-fronted boxes (p.31) and, occasionally, tit-boxes (p.26) and may use either of them for winter roosting. (Sometimes several wrens roost together to conserve heat.)

Bird-table Although a rare visitor, the wren takes tiny pieces of cake and breadcrumbs, especially from the ground. Sprinkle grated cheese among leaf litter as a special treat.

Hidden nest   A wren feeds its young at a nest in a wall, concealed behind tangled foliage.

Nesting information   Late April – July • 2 broods • 5 or 6 usually white eggs • 14–15 days incubation: female • 16–17 days fledging • 1–3 weeks until independent

WREN

Accentor family *(Prunellidae)*

DUNNOCK

Prunella modularis
Length: 14.5 cm (5¼ in)

Recognition
*The adult has a grey head, throat and breast.
(Juveniles are more striped.)*

YOU MIGHT OVERLOOK the dunnock (once known as the hedge sparrow) because its plumage is rather like the house sparrow's. However, the dunnock's shy, skulking habits, which keep it near cover, are very different. You may see the male flick both wings in courtship or give an aggressive display by quivering one wing.

Thin bill Compare with sparrows'

Ground-feeder
A dunnock feeds beneath a bird-table.

VOICE The song – warbling phrases, lasting four to five seconds – is similar to a wren's, only less powerful. The male has a repertoire of phrases copied from nearby dunnocks. The year-round song reaches a peak in March. A shrill *tseep* keeps a pair in touch.

FEEDING The diet is almost entirely seeds in winter and mainly sluggish insects in summer. The dunnock picks beetles, spiders, flies, caterpillars and bugs from plants or the ground.
Bird-table The dunnock sometimes comes to quiet bird-tables, but it feeds regularly on crumbs from the ground and occasionally on meat and seeds.

NESTING The nest of twigs and moss, lined with moss and hair, is built by the female in thick hedges, shrubs and evergreens. Dunnocks have a complex mating system, with males helping to feed the nestlings of each female with which they have mated.

Egg colour *Dunnocks are often foster parents to cuckoos. A cuckoo egg (right) contrasts with the dunnock's, but usually mimics other species' eggs.*

Nesting information April – August • 2 or 3 broods • 4 or 5 blue eggs • 14 days incubation: female • 12 days fledging • 2 weeks until independent

Warbler family *(Sylviidae)*

GOLDCREST

Regulus regulus
Length: 9 cm (3½ in)

THERE ARE RECORDS of the goldcrest, the smallest European bird, being trapped in spiders' webs. You may mistake goldcrests for tits, whose flocks they often join, as they search among foliage for insects and spiders. Once you have learnt the goldcrest's distinctive song and call notes, you will immediately recognize its presence in your garden.

VOICE The song is a thin, twittering *tweedly-tweedly-tweedly-twiddledidee*; the call is a thin *see-see*.

Short, needle-thin bill – *for picking up the tiniest of insects*

Olive-green above

Characteristic crest
The crest is yellow, bordered with black. Males display by spreading their crests, which are partly orange. (Juveniles lack the coloured crest.)

Wing-bars
There are two pale-coloured stripes on each wing.

FEEDING The goldcrest eats many kinds of spiders and insects, especially flies, aphids and beetles, and their larvae, but it occasionally takes larger types of insects, such as adult moths.
Bird-table Crumbs, fat and grated cheese are eaten, especially in bad weather.

Shelter By hunting under the dense foliage of evergreens, goldcrests can continue to find food even after a heavy snowfall.

NESTING Planting cypress, larch or other conifers will encourage goldcrests to nest, but they also use ivy and gorse. At the start of the breeding season, the males display by spreading their crests. You can easily overlook the goldcrest, not so much because of its small size but because it lives among leaves. The nest, mostly built by the female, is slung underneath foliage near the end of a branch. It is made of moss and lichen, held together and suspended with spiders' webs.

Nesting information April – July • 2 broods • 7–10 brown-spotted, white or buff eggs • 14–17 days incubation: female • 16–21 days fledging • Time until independent unknown

Flycatcher family *(Muscicapidae)*

SPOTTED FLYCATCHER

Muscicapa striata
Length: 14 cm (5½ in)

A SUMMER VISITOR, the spotted flycatcher is instantly recognizable by its feeding behaviour. It lives almost exclusively on flying insects, which it chases with an erratic, jinking flight from a large circuit of perches. Its need for winged insects restricts the spotted flycatcher's stay in Europe to the summer. If the weather is unseasonably cold or wet, flycatchers may have to rely on insects plucked off leaves or the ground.

Plumage *Light brown, streaked plumage sometimes appears almost grey. (Only juveniles are spotted.)*

VOICE Although usually unnoticed, the quiet song is a collection of squeaky notes. The call of a spotted flycatcher is a thin *see*.

FEEDING The spotted flycatcher usually feeds on flies, but also bees, butterflies and greenfly. Once a flycatcher has collected the insects in one area, it has to move to a new perch. After a period of time, it can return for more forays from the original perch.

Aerial pursuit
A flycatcher flits out to snap up an insect before returning to its perch.

NESTING Nesting starts after other insect-eaters, such as warblers and tits. The young are fledged at the height of summer when hot days make for active insect life. The nest of moss, grass and twigs, bound by cobwebs and lined with hair and feathers, is built mainly by the female, usually against a tree trunk or wall. An old nest may be used as a base.
Nest-box The flycatcher will use a bird-shelf (p.30) with a close perch.

Feeding the young *A flycatcher brings a small tortoiseshell butterfly to its nestlings.*

Nesting information *May–June* • *1 or 2 broods* • *4 or 5 brown-spotted, greenish eggs* • *12–14 days incubation: both sexes* • *12–13 days fledging* • *2–3 weeks until independent*

Thrush family *(Turdidae)*

FIELDFARE

Turdus pilaris
Length: 25 cm (10 in)

Recognition
The fieldfare is a large thrush distinguished by its grey head and rump and chestnut back.

I N WINTER, LOUD, chuckling calls will alert you to the sight of a ragged flock of large thrushes flying past. These are fieldfares, as much the heralds of winter as swallows are of summer. A cold spell and a fall of snow sets flocks in motion – this is the time that you are most likely to see fieldfares in your garden, together with redwings.

White underwings
(These flash in flight.)

VOICE The song is a medley of chuckles and whistles interspersed with *chacks*. The call is a harsh *chack-chack-chack*.

FEEDING The main fieldfare food is earthworms, snails and other small animals. Fruit is eaten in winter, especially when animal food is unavailable. Crops of berries, such as hawthorn, holly and rowan, and windfall apples are particular attractions. A single fieldfare will try to defend a tree against all comers.
Bird-table Fieldfares are keen on old, rotten fruit left out on the ground.

NESTING The fieldfare breeds in northern, central and eastern Europe, with only a few pairs nesting in northern Britain. The nest is a cup of grasses, twigs and mud, lined with fine grasses, built in a tree but sometimes on the ground. The nest is often exposed, but several pairs of birds build near each other and are aggressive towards intruders. People, cats and magpies coming too close are "dive-bombed" with angry cries and are sometimes spattered with droppings.

Winter fruit *If an apple is past its prime, store it somewhere dark. Come winter, fieldfares will be grateful for it.*

Rowan berries *– fieldfare food*

BIRD PROFILES

FIELDFARE

Nesting information *April – May • 1 or 2 broods • 4–6 red-speckled, pale blue eggs • 13–14 days incubation: female • 14 days fledging • 2 weeks until independent*

Thrush family *(Turdidae)*

ROBIN
Erithacus rubecula
Length: 14 cm (5½ in)

VOTED BRITAIN'S NATIONAL bird, the robin has spread into British gardens in a way that has not happened in the rest of Europe. Its natural habitat of woodland with a layer of undergrowth is mimicked by the hedges and shrubberies of British gardens. The roost is usually in dense vegetation, such as ivy, or in buildings and nest-boxes. Outside the breeding season, some robins join communal roosts.

Brown upper-parts and tail

Nightlife
The robin's large eyes seem to have good night vision because you often see or hear a robin in the garden when it is so dark that you can only recognize it by its plump outline.

Robin at night

Orange-red breast (absent in juveniles, which are spotted)

Territory Robins keep territories all year except during the moult period and the severest winter weather. Females usually defend their own separate territories in winter. A territory is needed not only for breeding but also to ensure a private food supply. Any robin without one will die within a few weeks, so defence of the territory is extremely aggressive. Usually the territory-owner only has to fluff out its red breast-feathers before the intruder retreats but rivals may come to blows and a fatal outcome is surprisingly common. If the thought of this is distressing, put out plenty of food, especially in hard weather.

VOICE You will hear bursts of liquid warbling all year. Both sexes sing to defend territory in winter. The male's more powerful spring song starts as early as December. Each robin may have several hundred different phrases. Alarm calls are a repeated *tic* and a thin *tseeee*.

Proclaiming territory
A robin declares its territory with a song.

FEEDING The robin mainly eats ground-living invertebrates – insects (especially beetles), snails, worms and spiders – but on rare occasions takes fish and tadpoles. From autumn to early spring, fruit and berries are an important part of the diet. Its chief method of hunting is well suited to the garden mixture of thick vegetation and open ground. The robin watches from a low perch, then drops down, seizes an

Catch and carry A robin brings insects to its young.

Winter food A robin appreciates a bowl of bread and cake crumbs in cold weather.

insect and flies up again. It also hops across the ground, pausing at intervals to watch for any moving prey. In their original habitat, robins followed pheasants, deer, wild boar and other large animals for any prey they disturbed. This is probably why robins in the garden are so trusting – they follow the gardener's spade as if it were the hoofs of a large mammal. Robins have even been known to follow moles working underground to catch worms escaping to the surface.
Bird-table Although mealworms are a great treat, robins eat any scraps of bread, meat, potatoes and fat. Some individuals take peanuts from hanging nets.

NESTING Robins pair up from December; usually the female joins the male on his territory. Pairing and nesting are earlier if the robins are well fed (bird-feeders help here). A hair-lined nest of moss and leaves, based on a pad of dead leaves, is built in a crevice in trees or in man-made objects, such as tins and letter-boxes. The male feeds the first family when the female lays another clutch.
Nest-box Open-fronted boxes (p.31) or sometimes tit-boxes with large holes.

Spring sight Young robins wait for food.

Nesting information April – July • 2 broods • 5 or 6 red-speckled, white or bluish eggs • 14 days incubation: female • 13–14 days fledging • 3 weeks until independent

Thrush family *(Turdidae)*

BLACKBIRD

Turdus merula
Length: 25 cm (10 in)

ALTHOUGH ORIGINALLY a bird of woodlands, the blackbird has become a successful garden bird because of its wide diet. The glossy, black male, with his bright yellow bill and eye-ring, is a familiar figure in the garden but the colours of the female and young birds may cause some confusion. By learning to identify the sex and age of blackbirds, you can make more sense of events in the garden. Pair-formation may start in the autumn before the nesting season, and you will often see territorial disputes, in which birds chase and attempt to fly up above one another.

ADULT MALE

Familiar glossy, black plumage

Juvenile male *A young male (left) gorges himself on cotoneaster berries. The juvenile male has a dull plumage (with a brownish hue, especially on the wings), a dark bill and no eye-ring until his first winter.*

VOICE The song consists of a couple of two-second phrases, often ending in a chuckle and sometimes interspersed with snatches of other birdsong as well as human whistles. You are most likely to hear the song of young males setting up their territories in February. It decreases after the eggs have been laid. A quiet subsong is heard in autumn. Several calls are heard for different situations, ranging from a subdued *pook-pook* when uneasy to a hysterical rattling when put to flight.

White bird
Blackbirds sometimes have a few white feathers.

Aggressive display *A blackbird threatens intruders away from its half-eaten apple with an aggressive open-beak display.*

Adult female *The female is dark brown, paler underneath, with faint spots and streaks.*

Pale eye-ring

Dark bill

FEEDING Fruit and berries (including cotoneaster, honeysuckle and barberry) are eaten in the latter half of the year, while earthworms, insects and other small animals are taken in spring and autumn. Caterpillars are an important food in summer but, as these are often rare in gardens, young are fed more on worms and adult insects. When hunting on a lawn, a blackbird cocks its head to one side before hopping forward to seize a worm from its burrow. It is not known whether the head posture helps the bird listen or look for earthworms (the latter is believed to be more likely). Blackbirds catch tadpoles and fish from ponds and steal food from other birds, such as large snails from song thrushes.

Bird-table Try putting out a variety of foods, including scraps, bread, fat, seeds and old fruit, such as apples and pears.

Rummaging for food *When foraging (right), one foot is raked backwards through dead leaves or loose soil as the bill flicks for food.*

NESTING The female builds a solid nest, usually in a shrub or hedge. Dry vegetation, which the male may help her collect, is reinforced with mud. The male sometimes stands guard over the eggs when the female is away feeding. The family is divided after fledging and each parent feeds particular youngsters, but the male may look after the whole family if the female has a new clutch to incubate.

Nest-box A large bird-shelf (p.30).

Leaf-lined nest *A lining of dead leaves or, usually, fine grasses distinguishes the blackbird's nest from that of the song thrush (p.67).*

Nesting information March – June • 3–5 broods • 3–5 brown-freckled, greenish-blue eggs • 13 days incubation: female • 13–14 days fledging • 3 weeks until independent

Thrush family *(Turdidae)*

SONG THRUSH

Turdus philomelos
Length: 23 cm (9 in)

Recognition
The song thrush is a warmer brown than the mistle thrush.

A REGULAR GARDEN VISITOR, the song thrush is more often seen feeding on the lawn and in flowerbeds than at the bird-table. It is one of the best garden songsters and its far-carrying whistling, unlike the blackbird's song, can be heard almost all year round. Its loud contribution to the dawn chorus that you hear on mild winter mornings is linked to the defence of territories. In cold weather, or if food is otherwise in short supply, song thrushes living in the countryside may join those already in gardens.

VOICE The song is composed of clear, fluting phrases, usually repeated three or four times, and delivered from a tree-top perch. A call note *tick* is given in flight and there are blackbird-like notes of alarm (p.64). As summer advances, you may hear fledged young calling to their parents with sharp *chicks* from their hideouts in the undergrowth.

Wings *The orange flash beneath each wing distinguishes the song thrush from the mistle thrush (p.68) and fieldfare. The redwing has an even more obvious flash.*

Tree-top perch

FEEDING The song thrush feeds on insects and other invertebrates. Worms are an important food, especially in the earlier part of the year, as is fruit (including fallen apples, and elder, holly and rowan berries) in autumn. Snails are an emergency ration, mostly taken in winter frosts or summer droughts when hard ground makes worms difficult to come by. To break open the snails' protective shells, song thrushes dash them against a hard "anvil", such as a stone, path or tree root. Breaking shells and sorting through the

Distinctive feeding method *The song thrush hops or runs forward, occasionally pauses to look for prey (with its head cocked to one side) and then pounces, often on an earthworm.*

Yew berries *Song thrushes eat the red, fleshy fruits without digesting the poisonous seeds.*

untidy remains is a laborious and time-consuming task that is not worthwhile when other food is readily available. Only song thrushes smash open snails but watch for blackbirds waiting to snatch the snail flesh from them.

Bird-table Shyness often keeps the song thrush from the bird-table but it does feed underneath, taking fat, sultanas and kitchen scraps. It appreciates apples left in quiet corners, near to the cover offered by hedges and shrubs.

Snail smashing *A tapping noise may reveal the presence of a song thrush in the garden. To get at the soft flesh, the thrush grips the lip of the snail's shell and batters it against an anvil.*

Snail remains
Broken shells litter the anvil.

NESTING The female constructs the solid, cup-shaped nest from grasses, leaves, roots and twigs embedded in earth. The smooth nest lining, of dung or mud mixed with saliva, is a trademark of the song thrush. A well-shaded site is usually chosen for the nest: low in a bush, tree or among the thick foliage of creepers, such as ivy. The same nest may be re-used for further broods.

Mud-lined nest *The smooth mud lining that stiffens the song thrush's bulky nest may sometimes be missing in dry summers.*

Nesting information *March–August • 2 or 3 broods • 4–6 black-spotted, blue eggs • 13–14 days incubation: female • 26–28 days fledging • 3 weeks until independent*

Thrush family (*Turdidae*)

MISTLE THRUSH

Turdus viscivorus
Length: 27 cm (10½ in)

VOICE Song is a far-carrying, ringing variation of *tee-tor-tee-tor-tee*. A harsh, rattling call is given when alarmed.

T HE LARGEST EUROPEAN thrush, the aggressive mistle thrush requires a large territory so it is never abundant. It is so named because it feeds on mistletoe. In Great Britain, where mistletoe is less common, the species used to be known as the holly thrush because of its fondness for the deep red berries of holly bushes.

Recognition
Larger than the song thrush, the mistle thrush has greyer plumage.

FEEDING A wide range of insects and fruit is eaten. In early winter, the loose flocks break up and mistle thrushes defend territories around crops of mistletoe, yew, hawthorn or holly from other birds.
Bird-table Kitchen scraps, bread and apples. Mistle thrushes may defend a bird-table supply from other visitors.

Take off Pale underwings contrast with the song thrush's flash.

Holly berries

NESTING The female takes one to two weeks to build a grass-lined nest of earth and plants, usually in a fork of a tree. Cats, birds of prey and people that come too close to the nest are attacked. Once fledged, the juveniles form small flocks.

Two broods Although both adult birds feed the nestlings initially, the male continues to feed the first brood on his own once the female lays her second clutch.

Nesting information Late February – July • 2 broods • 4 speckled, whitish eggs • 12–15 days incubation: female • 12–15 days fledging • 2 weeks until independent

Long-tailed tit family *(Aegithalidae)*

LONG-TAILED TIT

Aegithalos caudatus
Length: 14 cm (5¹/₂ in)

Recognition *The plumage is mainly black and white. (Juveniles are browner.)*

Long tail

VOICE
There is no proper song, but a sharp *tsirrup* and thin, repeated *zee* are given in flight and a short *pit* when perched.

YOU ARE MOST likely to see parties of long-tailed tits passing through the garden rather than visiting a bird-table. The flocks mainly comprise parents and their offspring of the year. Apart from helping each other to find food and avoid predators, the flock members huddle together on cold nights to keep warm. In February or March, winter parties disband and males set up their own territories within the flock territory and mate with females from other flocks.

Pinkish tinge on body

FEEDING Long-tailed tits eat far fewer seeds than other tits and mainly take insects and other invertebrates. They are agile in their search of leaves and twigs, but, unlike other tits, do not hold food under the foot while pecking at it. Instead, they hang upside down by one foot while clutching the food in the other.

NESTING Nest-building starts in February or March and takes about three weeks because the nest is extremely elaborate. The ball of moss, spiders' webs, hair, feathers and lichen is built by both sexes in a bush, bramble thicket, hedge or high in a fork of a tree. The nestlings are sometimes fed by helpers. These are close relatives who have lost their own nests to predators.

Feather lining *The hundreds of feathers that are added to the nest make the lining so snug that when the female is incubating she has to fold her tail over her back to fit inside.*

Bird-table Some long-tailed tits form the habit of visiting, especially when ice locks up natural food. They prefer small fragments of meat, fat and peanuts and are tempted by fat smeared on to the bark of trees.

Spider – a favoured natural food

Nesting information *March – May • 1 brood • 8–12 reddish-freckled, white eggs • 14–18 days incubation: female • 15–16 days fledging • Independent at next nesting season*

69

Tit family *(Paridae)*

BLUE TIT
Parus caeruleus
Length: 11.5 cm (4½ in)

T HE BLUE TIT is one of the most delightful birds to visit
the birdfeeder because of its bold, perky behaviour
and the skilful acrobatics it performs on nut bags and
tit-bells. One of the most frequent users of
the bird-table, the blue tit is credited
with high intelligence, partly due to its
habit of investigating new sources of
food and using its dexterity of foot and
beak to obtain them. Studies with ringed birds
have shown that over 100 blue tits may visit a
garden in succession, although only a few can be
seen at one time. Not many travel more than
six miles on their daily round, although
some migrate over 60 miles from their
summer breeding-grounds.

Recognition You can tell a blue tit by the
bright blue on its cap and wings. (Juveniles
are generally duller and have yellow cheeks.)

VOICE The blue tit song is *tsee-tsee-tsu-
hu-hu-hu*, which is used to keep in contact,
a harsh *tsee* and a *churr* of alarm.

Blue wings

Fast food The content of your nut bag
decreases rapidly if blue tits can pull out whole
peanuts and carry them away to eat at leisure.

Threat posture
In an aggressive display,
a blue tit threatens other
birds by raising the
feathers on its
head to make
it look bigger.

*Bright
blue cap*

*White
cheeks*

*Bright yellow
underparts*

Keeping clean As well as being a
frequent visitor to the bird-table, the
blue tit also enjoys using a bird-bath.

An apple a day
When blue tits feed on windfall apples, they are not only interested in eating the fruit's flesh but will tunnel through it to reach the seeds.

FEEDING The diet comprises insects in summer and a mixture of insects and seeds, especially beech mast, in winter. Buds are stripped in search of small insects – aphids and weevils are often eaten but caterpillars provide the bulk of food needed for rearing the nestlings. Blue tits sometimes visit willow catkins and the flowers of gooseberries, currants and other garden plants for nectar. A natural resourcefulness enables blue tits to take advantage of changing crops, while their tameness allows them to exploit food deliberately or unwittingly left out. Once a feeding method has been adapted to suit a new food, blue tits quickly learn from each other, as happened with their habit of stealing milk.

Bird-table Peanuts, seeds, fruit, fat, meat and assorted scraps are eaten. The blue tit is one of the most agile garden birds and is fun to watch as it feeds on hanging baskets, tit-bells, suet sticks, halved coconuts or strings of peanuts.

Seeds (right) – one of the many foods that attract blue tits

Table-talk *Blue tits (left) squabble over their shares of a bird pudding.*

NESTING Nest-building starts with the female chipping at the entrance of a hole or crevice (even if it is a suitably sized hole in a nest-box). The time taken to collect material and build the nest varies from a few days to several weeks, if work is held up by bad weather. The nest of moss, dried grasses and small twigs is lined with fine grasses and feathers.
Nest-box Blue tits are among the most frequent users of tit-boxes (p.26).

Large clutch *One egg was laid each morning until this clutch of 10 eggs was complete.*

Nesting information *March – June • 1 or 2 broods • 5–12 reddish-flecked, white eggs • 14 days incubation: female • 18 days fledging • 4 weeks until independent*

Tit family *(Paridae)*

GREAT TIT

Parus major
Length: 14 cm (5½ in)

Greyish-blue and green upperparts

D UE TO ITS readiness to use a nest-box, the great tit is one of the best studied of all birds. By saturating an area with nest-boxes almost the entire population of great tits can be persuaded to nest, allowing the progress of their breeding to be monitored easily. Natural nest holes in trees are scarcer in gardens than woods, so tit-boxes have a strong chance of being used by some of the great tits that have regularly attended the birdfeeders in your garden through the winter.

Recognition *You can recognize the great tit by its size – it is the largest member of the tit family.*

Gender gap *You can easily distinguish the female by her narrower black breast-stripe and less glossy plumage. Noticing the difference shows you that males dominate at feeders.*

VOICE In late winter, depending on the mildness of the weather, great tits start associating in pairs and become more vocal. A male sings most intensely to acquire a mate but, until the young have flown, he will also sing to advertise his territory. Great tits have one of the largest vocal repertoires of any small bird. Each tit's song incorporates several different phrases, which are variations on a basic phrase, described as *teacher-teacher* or a squeaky bicycle pump. With practice, it is possible to differentiate between individuals. Perhaps not surprisingly, the tits also recognize each other's songs and do not react to the familiar song of a neighbour, whose presence next to their territory they have come to

Black and white head

Bright yellow belly

Broad breast-stripe

Dominant male *The male whose territory encompasses the bird-table will chivvy visiting great tits – they are allowed on to the birdfeeder as long as they know their place and do not attempt to assert themselves.*

Calls Great tits have a range of calls: birdwatchers say that if you cannot identify the call of a garden bird, it is sure to be a great tit!

accept. However, territory-owners will respond immediately to a stranger's song because it represents a dangerous intrusion into their property.

There is an amazing variety of calls: the great tit's most familiar *pink* call is given by territory-holders and a churring note is given when disturbed. In late summer, the sibilant *tsee-tsee-tsee* calls give away the presence of youngsters that have only recently left the nest.

Insect hunt A great tit climbs up a tree to search and probe for insects.

Tail – used as support

Hazelnuts – enjoyed by great tits

FEEDING Winter food for great tits is largely tree seeds, such as beech mast and even hazelnuts. Great tits are not as agile as other tits and spend more time feeding on the ground. Summer food is mainly insects, especially weevils, but also spiders and small snails.

Bird-table Peanuts, seeds, meat bones and fat. Hanging peanut bags, scrap baskets or halved coconuts filled with bird pudding allow you the opportunity to observe the antics of great tits.

NESTING The female builds the nest of moss in the hollow or cleft of a tree, or in a hole in a wall, and lines it with hair. The amount of time during which the fledglings continue to be fed depends on whether or not there is another brood, although a second clutch is a rare event.

Nest-box Large and standard-sized tit-boxes (p.26). The great tit is one of the most common users of nest-boxes.

Delivering food A great tit returns to its nest hole with food (usually moth caterpillars) for its hungry young family.

Nesting information April – July • 1 or 2 broods • 5–12 reddish-spotted, white eggs • 13–14 days incubation: female • 18–20 days fledging • 1–2 weeks until independent

Tit family *(Paridae)*
COAL TIT
Parus ater
Length: 11 cm (4¼ in)

Pine

Black cap and white cheeks

T HE COAL TIT does not use bird-tables and nest-boxes as often as blue and great tits and is less likely to leave its woodland home in winter, only visiting suburbs if there is a food shortage. The coal tit is most at home among conifers – its long toes make it easy to grip bunches of conifer needles.

Long toes

VOICE The song is *teachoo-teachoo* – similar to the great tit's song, but higher-pitched. The *tsee-tsee* call resembles that of a goldcrest.

Recognition *Identify the coal tit by the white stripe on its nape.*

FEEDING Using its slender beak, the coal tit probes crevices for tiny insects, or extracts seeds from cones in winter. Seeds, nuts and even insects are hoarded. A coal tit may empty a hopper of seeds, causing some plants to grow in odd places.
Bird-table Peanuts, seeds and fat.

Slender beak
The beak, longer than that of other tits, is better for carrying nuts.

NESTING The nest is made in a hollow or cleft, usually low in a tree, or in a mouse-hole if no tree sites are available. The nest of moss is usually lined with hair, (distinguishing it from the (usually feather-lined) nest of a blue tit (p.71).
Nest-box A coal tit will use a tit-box (p.26), especially if placed on a conifer.

Begging for food *Fully feathered nestlings in a tree-hole nest gape to receive caterpillars.*

Nesting information *April – June • 1 or 2 broods • 7–12 reddish-spotted, white eggs • 17–18 days incubation: female • 16 days fledging • 2 weeks until independent*

Nuthatch family *(Sittidae)*

NUTHATCH

Sitta europaea

Length: 14 cm (5½ in)

Awl-shaped beak

T HE NUTHATCH IS a woodland bird that visits gardens with mature trees. It usually feeds high in the canopy, where it gives away its presence by loud, cheerful calls, but it is a frequent visitor to the bird-table. In autumn and winter, nuthatches feed among flocks of tits.

VOICE The song is a rapid, trilling *chi-chi-chi*, heard mostly from January to May. The loud, ringing *chit-chit* call is heard all year round.

Recognition
The nuthatch has a streamlined body, short tail and black eye-stripe.

FEEDING The nuthatch probes crevices for spiders and insects. From autumn onwards, hazelnuts, acorns and beechnuts are wedged firmly into holes and hammered open by the powerful, awl-shaped beak, making a tapping noise that can be mistaken for a woodpecker chipping at the tree. Some nuts are stored in crevices.
  Bird-table Peanuts, sunflower seeds, cake and fat-smeared tree trunks.

Sign of a nuthatch
A hazelnut shell lies wedged in the bark of an oak tree, after having been opened.

Headfirst
Woodpeckers and treecreepers only move up trees, using their tails as props, but the nuthatch can hop down with equal skill.

NESTING Both sexes choose a hole in a tree or wall or take an abandoned nest. They plaster the entrance with mud or dung (probably to reduce the hole size and prevent larger birds taking over) and line the hollow with leaves or bark flakes.
Nest-box Enclosed nest-box (p.31).

Sealed *Mud has been plastered on to a box.*

Nesting information *Late April – June • 1 brood • 6–9 reddish-spotted, white eggs •*
14–15 days incubation: female • 23–25 days fledging • Several days until independent

Treecreeper family *(Certhiidae)*

TREECREEPER

Certhia familiaris
Length: 12.5 cm (5 in)

Long, down-curved beak

GARDENS WITH MATURE trees will attract treecreepers, especially in winter. Unlike nuthatches and tits, which also search bark for food, treecreepers do not hang head-down and only hop upwards, using their strong tails as props like miniture woodpeckers. Inspect the trunks of dead trees: streaks of droppings mark roost sites.

VOICE The song is a thin, sibilant succession of notes ending in a little flourish: *see-see-see-sissi-sooee,* reminiscent of a loud goldcrest or high-pitched chaffinch. The repeated *see* and *sit* call notes are often thin and difficult to hear.

Fledgling (Adults have longer tails.)

Searching
The tree-creeper flies to a base of a tree, hunting for insects as it climbs up.

FEEDING The diet is almost entirely small insects and spiders plucked from bark – rarely from foliage or the ground.
Bird-table Treecreepers may come to the bird-table but are more surely attracted if you smear a mixture of chopped nuts and porridge, or fat, over bark or into holes.

NESTING Both sexes build a nest from twigs, grasses and moss and line it with feathers. They place it behind a flap of bark or the cladding of a building, in a crevice or hollow, or occasionally in dense vegetation, such as ivy. Once fledged, family parties often join tits and goldcrests in mixed flocks.
Nest-box A specially designed, wedge-shaped box (p.28) is sometimes used if natural nest sites are scarce.

Chick-rearing An adult bird feeds a moth to its young. The nest is located behind some loose bark on a tree trunk.

Nesting information April – June • 1 or 2 broods • 5–7 brown-spotted, white eggs •
14–15 days incubation: female • *14–15 days fledging* • *Time until independent unknown*

Finch family *(Fringillidae)*

CHAFFINCH
Fringilla coelebs
Length: 15 cm (6 in)

THE CHAFFINCH IS a woodland bird but it is also common in gardens and parks where tall trees provide food and song-posts. In good years, flocks of chaffinches gather under beech trees to feed on beech mast. Study the birds carefully to see if any of the closely related bramblings (which have orange bodies) are among them.

MALE

Conspicuous white flashes on wings and tail

VOICE The song is a regular series of repeated notes that ends with a flourish: *chip-chip-chip-chuwee-chuwee-tissichooee.* The call is a sharp *pink-pink.*

Plumage In spring, the cock chaffinch's buff feather tips wear away to reveal the brighter colours of the breeding plumage.

Breeding plumage – a colourful mixture of pink, chestnut and slate-blue

Female The hen resembles a female sparrow, but look for white on wings and tail.

FEEDING The chaffinch mainly eats seeds that have fallen on the ground, including beech mast, cereal grains, chickweeds and charlock. The parents feed the young on caterpillars, flies, spiders and other small animals.
Bird-table Chaffinches eat a variety of seeds and scraps, often picking up spillings under the bird-table rather than landing on it themselves.

NESTING The female builds a delicate nest, mostly of grass and moss, in a tree fork. It is lined with feathers and rootlets and decorated on the outside with lichens and spiders' webs. The female takes over a thousand trips to gather the nest material. The male accompanies her as she works but does not help.

*Patient fledgling
A fledgling chaffinch waits for food among flowering oak. During the breeding season, adult birds switch to collecting insects to feed their young.*

Nesting information May – August • 1 or 2 broods • 3–5 purple-marked, blue eggs • 12–14 days incubation: female • 12–14 days fledging • 2–3 weeks until independent

Finch family *(Fringillidae)*

GOLDFINCH

Carduelis carduelis
Length: 12 cm (4¾ in)

THIS JEWEL OF a bird is less likely to visit a well-kept garden. The best way to attract goldfinches is to ensure a crop of seeding thistles, dandelions, groundsel or sowthistles, although they have also started to feed at peanut bags. A small flock of goldfinches energetically attacking seed heads is a delightful sight. If you see a goldfinch on teazel, it is likely to be male because the slightly duller female, whose bill is fractionally shorter, has difficulty extracting the seeds. Goldfinches may take the seeds of garden plants such as lavender.

Seed-head specialist
The slender bill is ideal for probing for seeds.

VOICE The call is a liquid *switt-witt-witt* and the song is a twittering, rambling variation on these notes.

Bold patches of yellow and red

FEEDING Large teazel, thistle and burdock seeds are preferred but when they run out the goldfinch eats the smaller groundsel, dandelion, ragwort or sowthistle seeds. It also eats the seeds of elm, birch and pine.
Bird-table Peanuts and cage-bird seeds, such as millet, are eaten.

Teazel
The seeds lie at the bottom of long tubes, surrounded by bristles.

Duller fledgling
The juvenile has a streaked, grey-brown body and is less colourful on the head. Buff feathers conceal the distinctive gold wing-bar.

NESTING The female builds a cup-nest of moss, roots and lichens, lined with wool and thistle-down, often near the end of a branch. The territories are small and several pairs of birds may nest close to each other. Courtship involves both sexes spreading their wings and tails to show off their colourful plumage.

Nesting information April – August • 2 or 3 broods • 4–6 red-freckled, white eggs • 11–13 days incubation: female • 13–16 days fledging • 2 weeks until independent

Finch family *(Fringillidae)*

GREENFINCH

Carduelis chloris
Length: 14.5 cm (5³/₄ in)

T HE GREENFINCH HAS become
more common in gardens
as it gradually colonized towns and
cities during this century. This is
partly because of the loss of grain
and weed seeds due to intensive
farming, but the greenfinch has
also changed habitat to exploit
peanuts and sunflower seeds in feeders.

VOICE The male's rasping *sweee* betrays
greenfinches hidden in foliage. The song
is a medley of notes ending in a loud
wheeze. A repeated *chi-chi-chi-chi* is
given in flight.

Recognition
*Greenfinches have green
and yellow plumage. The female is duller.*

*Yellow
wing-patches*
*These distinguish
females from
sparrows.*

FEEDING The diet comprises a wide
assortment of seeds, including elm,
yew, bramble, dandelion and burdock.
Bird-table As well as feeding on peanuts
and sunflower seeds in hoppers and
hanging bags, greenfinches also gather
on the ground underneath bird-tables
or nearby perches to collect the seed
fragments dropped by other birds.

NESTING Greenfinches, unlike most
other birds, remain sociable through the
breeding season . They nest in small colonies of about half a dozen pairs, usually
in a dense shrub. The female builds the
nest of twigs, grass and moss and lines
it with hair and rootlets.

Mixed diet *Nestlings stretch and gape as a
parent returns. Caterpillars and aphids are
important for nestlings, but the young receive
only regurgitated seeds once they leave the nest.*

Nesting information April – August • 2 or 3 broods • 4 – 6 red-spotted, white eggs •
12 – 14 days incubation: female • 13 – 16 days fledging • 2 weeks until independent

Finch family *(Fringillidae)*

SISKIN

Carduelis spinus
Length: 12 cm (4¾ in)

Grey-green plumage

A NEWCOMER TO GARDENS over the last 30 years, the siskin is a small finch with the acrobatic habits of a tit. It searches for food at the tips of slender twigs, where it hangs upside-down as it pecks at cones and bunches of seeds. The favourite foods of the siskin are the seeds of birch, alder and conifers. The siskin was probably first attracted to gardens by the planting of ornamental conifers, such as cypress. It is now a regular winter visitor and comes into gardens especially when natural seed crops are exhausted.

FEMALE

Yellow rump and sides of tail

Forked tail

Recognition *The female is greenish-yellow, with dark streaks beneath. The male (below) has a black cap and bib, is less streaked and generally brighter.*

VOICE The song is a twittering, ending in a wheeze. The calls are a *tsooee* and a twitter given on the wing.

Alder catkins and cones

Black cap

Yellow wing-bars

MALE

FEEDING Siskins take seeds from spruce and pine cones as well as alder, birch, elm, thistles and dock. Insects are fed to growing nestlings.
Bird-table Peanuts, fat and a variety of seeds. For some unknown reason, the siskin is particularly attracted to peanuts in red plastic mesh bags, or other red containers.

NESTING The female builds the tidy, compact nest from small, lichen-covered twigs and lines it with rootlets, hair and feathers. It is usually sited near the end of a branch, high off the ground in a conifer. Recent, widespread plantations of conifers throughout Europe have increased the species' range.

Nesting information *May – August • 2 broods • 3–5 red-streaked, pale blue eggs • 12 days incubation: female • 15 days fledging • Time until independent unknown*

Finch family *(Fringillidae)*

BULLFINCH

Pyrrhula pyrrhula
Length: 14.5 cm (5³/₄ in)

Willow catkins – spring food

Black cap

White rump

T HE BULLFINCH CAN easily pass unnoticed in the garden because it keeps to thick foliage. Even if you flush one out, often all you catch sight of is a flash of white rump. There are many gardeners who dislike bullfinches because of the damage they can do in spring to fruit-tree buds and blossom and, later, to soft fruit and peas. The bullfinch's preferred winter diet is seeds but when stocks run out it turns to eating buds, even though these contain little nourishment.

MALE

Recognition The male has deep pink under- parts. (The female is greyer.)

FEMALE

Greyish underparts

FEEDING Bullfinches mainly eat the seeds of ash, birch, dock, nettle and bramble, but they also rip buds off trees. During the breeding season insects are fed to the nestlings.
Bird-table Bullfinches occasionally feed on peanuts and assorted seeds.

VOICE The song is a quiet warbling. The call is a distinc- tive whistling *deu-deu*, which you can hear plainly, even when the birds are hidden.

NESTING Unlike most other garden birds, pairs stay together through the year rather than split up after breeding. In spring, the male takes the initiative in choosing the nest site. He leads the female to suitable locations in a thick hedge or conifer but she builds the delicate nest of fine twigs and rootlets.

Fledgling A bullfinch, just out of the nest, perches among rose hips. It has brownish plumage and lacks the distinctive black cap.

Nesting information April – August • 2 broods • 4 or 5 purple-streaked, green-blue eggs • 14 days incubation: female • 12–16 days fledging • 2–3 weeks until independent

Sparrow family *(Passeridae)*

HOUSE SPARROW

Passer domesticus
Length: 14.5 cm (5¼ in)

THE HOUSE SPARROW deserves its name. It rarely nests away from buildings, although it occasionally nests in holes in trees and rock faces, or usurps the nests of other birds, such as martins and swallows. Less often, it makes its own domed nest of grasses in a tree or hedge. Exploiting human settlements for shelter and food has enabled house sparrows to spread all over the world.

MALE

Black bib

Recognition
The male has brown upper-parts, streaked with black, and grey cheeks, crown and rump.

Other sparrows Watch out for tree sparrows: unlike the house sparrow, they lack the grey crown and rump, and have a brown spot in the middle of each cheek.

VOICE The house sparrow has a variety of persistent *cheep* and *chirp* calls, and a song that is a medley of these calls.

Song A male (left) chirps monotonously to try to attract a mate.

Garden disturbance A common sight in spring is a group of sparrows chasing each other across the garden, chirruping wildly, and ending up in a tree where they mill about, apparently fighting. It is difficult to see precisely what is happening but the object of excitement is a female and the other participants are males who are courting her. She will try to fend them off, aided by her mate.

Centre of attention *The female is more uniformly brown, lacking the grey on rump and crown and the black on the head and throat. (Juveniles resemble the female.)*

FEMALE

Nettle *The common stinging nettle, although trouble for the gardener, will provide a meal of seeds for the house sparrow.*

FEEDING The house sparrow is basically a seed-eater but it eats a wide mixture of animal and plant food, including shoots and flowers. House sparrows are pests on farms, stealing grain from standing crops, and wherever they have access to human food. Urban sparrows used to rely on grain spilt from horses' nosebags but they now do well on the increasing amount of edible litter. Animal food is needed for feeding to the nestlings. Look out for house sparrows chasing flies across the lawn, gorging on greenfly and even picking insects out of spiders' webs.

Nutrition *A female sparrow takes some scraps of food from a hanging basket.*

Seed-eaters *House sparrows feed on seeds and edible litter in a city park.*

NESTING The usual nesting site is a hole or crevice in a building. Thatched houses provide attractive sites, so wire netting is used to keep sparrows from burrowing into the thatch. After nesting has finished, pairs of house sparrows continue to use the nest as a snug roost throughout the winter. (The young birds roost together in evergreens and among ivy. You can see them gathering in late afternoon and hear them twittering conversationally in the foliage until darkness falls.)

Nest-box House sparrows readily use enclosed nest-boxes (p.31) and may even displace tits from them.

Bird-table House sparrows can be a problem in gardens because flocks clear bird-tables of all forms of scraps. Despite this, there is much of interest in their habits. They are quick to learn new ways of finding food, following the example of tits in stealing milk from bottles and learning to feed from tit-bells and peanut bags.

Feathering the nest *A male perches on a wire with material for his nest, which may be built in a hole in a building.*

Nesting information March – September • 2– 4 broods • 3–5 brown-blotched, white eggs • 14 days incubation: mainly female • 15 days fledging • 1 week until independent

Starling family *(Sturnidae)*

STARLING

Sturnus vulgaris
Length: 22 cm (8½ in)

T HE STARLING IS SO widespread that fruit-growers consider it a pest, as do people in cities because it fouls buildings on which it roosts. A bold nature coupled with a voracious appetite has not made starlings popular in the garden, because they clear the bird-table before other birds can claim their share. Yet their lively behaviour makes starlings attractive birds to watch as they perform a repertoire of fascinating activities.

Recognition In winter, starlings have spangled plumage. This starling in its first winter has lost the mouse-brown juvenile plumage.

Buff-speckled above

Glossy plumage

White-speckled below

Scene at dusk Just before dusk, you can see large numbers of starlings meeting in trees before they fly to their communal roost.

Flight In summer, starlings hawk for flying insects. Pointed wings and a short, square tail give the starling an arrowhead silhouette in flight.

Flocks For much of the year starlings live in flocks. They feed together, so there is often a rush of starlings to the bird-table. After breeding, thousands swarm to join vast communal roosts. In the evening, you can hear a chorus of noisy squeals as they fly overhead in close formation.

Plumage The starling's glossy, blackish feathers are shot with metallic blues, purples and greens. After the summer moult, the buff and white tips to new feathers create an attractive, spangled appearance, most marked in young birds.

Spring plumage The plumage has lost much of its spotted appearance because the pale tips of the feathers have worn away.

Long, pointed beak
(brown in winter)

Singing out *A male sings,
throat-feathers raised and
wings flapping, from a
prominent perch to
attract a mate to
his nest site.*

VOICE The song is a medley of rattles, squeaks and whistles, often with mimicked notes of other species, including curlew, pheasant and tawny owl. When singing at high intensity, the throat-feathers are raised and part-spread wings are waved. Singing occurs at communal roosts as well as in the territory. Calls include an aggressive *chacker-chacker* and a harsh, screaming distress call.

Lawn food *A starling extracts a leatherjacket.*

Bird-table Put out bread, scraps, hanging bones and peanut bags for starlings.

NESTING The male builds a rough nest of grass, which is lined by the female, in a hole in a tree or building. He may also decorate it with green leaves and flower petals collected from plants with insecticidal properties. The drawback with open-beak feeding (described above) is that to collect a good beakful for the nestlings, a starling has to drop one item of food before probing for the next. Later, fledglings are brought to the lawn and food is crammed directly into their beaks.
Nest-box Large enclosed box (p.31).

FEEDING Starlings visit the garden for a wide variety of animal and plant foods. Their main food is earthworms, leatherjackets (the larvae of craneflies) and other small creatures found near grass roots. They stride forward in a group, inspecting the ground with frequent, rapid thrusts of their beaks. The beak is equipped with strong muscles for forcing it open at each probe into the soil. Swivelling its eyes forwards to peer down the hole, the starling will focus on the end of its beak to identify anything worth eating. At the same time, it is still able to scan around for any lurking predators, such as cats.

Meal-time *A parent brings small insects and spiders to its young beneath the roof of a house.*

Nesting information April – May • 1 or 2 broods • 4 or 5 pale greenish-blue eggs •
12 days incubation: female • 21 days fledging • 4–5 weeks until independent

Crow family *(Corvidae)*

JAY
Garrulus glandarius
Length: 34 cm (13½ in)

T HE MOST COLOURFUL member of the crow family, the jay is becoming a regular visitor to rural and suburban gardens where there are plenty of mature trees. It is often shy and, in its natural woodland home, usually gives away its presence only by its harsh *krar* cries, but it may be seen as it flaps jerkily and heavily across clearings on its broad wings. Jays visit bird-tables most readily in the early morning before people are about.

Pale blue wing-patch

Streaked crown
The crown can be raised into a crest, giving a domed appearance to the head.

VOICE Rasping *krar* sounds are used as alarm calls and in social inter-actions. There are a number of quieter guttural and warbling notes. Jays are good mimics and imitate other crows, tawny owls and even birdsong.

White rump

Pinkish-fawn body

Flight When flying away, black wings and tail contrast with the white rump and white and pale blue wing-patches.

Retrieving acorns
Jays bury surplus acorns and can remember where they have been buried even through 30 cm (12 in) of snow.

FEEDING Acorns are the important food for most of the year. Jays also eat other seeds and fruit, as well as insects (in particular, beetles and caterpillars) and occasionally mice and voles.
Bird-table Jays come for vegetable scraps, which they carry away to eat or bury. Some have learnt to take peanuts from mesh bags or wire spiral dispensers.

NESTING Both sexes build the untidy nest in a tree or tall shrub, usually at some height above the ground. It is mainly composed of twigs broken off trees, bound together with earth, and lined with roots, hair and fibres. Jays sometimes rob small birds' nests, perhaps only when they have young to feed.

Nesting information May – June • 1 brood • 3–7 brown-flecked, greenish eggs • 16–17 days incubation: female • 21–23 days fledging • 8 weeks until independent

---

Crow family *(Corvidae)*

MAGPIE

Pica pica
Length: 46 cm (18 in)

Plumage *There is a greenish gloss to the black and white feathers.*

THE MOST UNPOPULAR garden bird, the magpie is damned for keeping watch on garden song-birds to locate their nests and then ravage them. Yet it is unfair to single out the magpie as even tits and thrushes occasionally kill other birds. A magpie "wedding" starts when a pair tries to carve out a new territory from an established one. The residents attempt to drive the interlopers out and the noise of the chase attracts other magpies.

VOICE A harsh *kyack* or a repeated *shak-shak-shak* of alarm is often the first sign of a magpie's presence.

20–25 cm (8–10 in) long tail

Scrap
A magpie feeds on meat

FEEDING
Like most crows, the magpie eats almost anything: beetles, grasshoppers, slugs, snails, woodlice and spiders, and many seeds and fruit. The nestlings of other birds, animal road casualties and injured birds are easy meals. **Bird-table** Meat and bread scraps.

NESTING The nest is a substantial structure of sticks and twigs, lined with mud and plant material, and is usually built in a tree or tall shrub. In areas of Europe, magpies nest on buildings or electricity pylons. The family stays near the nest for several days after fledging. The young remain in a loose flock.

Magpie nest
The domed nest has a single side-opening and is roofed over with thorns as a protection against predatory attacks by other crows.

Nesting information March – May • 1 or 2 broods • 5–7 speckled, greenish eggs •
22 days incubation: female • 22–27 days fledging • Time until independent unknown

Crow family *(Corvidae)*

CARRION CROW

Corvus corone
Length: 47 cm (18¹/₂ in)

Strong, black bill

Lıke other members of the crow family, the carrion crow is shy of people. If not persecuted, it becomes tame enough to search for food in gardens, which unfortunately includes the eggs and nestlings of small birds. While adult crows live in their territories, the non-breeding young gather in flocks. The carrion crow may interbreed with the hooded crow, a race of the carrion crow (distinguished by its grey body) which lives in northern and western Europe, including Scotland and Ireland.

Recognition The carrion crow is all black, without the bare, grey face of the rook.

VOICE There is a number of caws. A repeated *kraa-kraa-kraa* is the male's "song" and is given while jerking the head up and spreading the tail. You can hear an angry *ark-ark* during territorial disputes, and a longer *kaaar* when the crow is alarmed.

Acorn – part of a varied diet

FEEDING The crow eats a broad range of food, including carrion, grain, acorns, potatoes, insects and their larvae, snails, worms and the eggs and nestlings of other birds. Surplus food is hoarded.
Bird-table Bread, meat, potatoes and other kitchen scraps attract crows.

NESTING The substantial nest, built by both sexes high in a tree fork, is made of three layers: an outer cup of twigs; a middle layer of fine twigs, roots, earth and

Hunting A crow scans the lawn for worms.

grass; and a lining of hair and bark fibres. While the female incubates the eggs, the male stands guard, warning her of danger as well as bringing food to her.

Nesting information *March – June • 1 brood • 4 or 5 brown-speckled, greenish eggs •*
17–19 days incubation: female • 32–36 days fledging • 4 weeks until independent

Crow family *(Corvidae)*

ROOK

Corvus frugilegus
Length: 46 cm (18 in)

SUPERFICIALLY SIMILAR TO the carrion crow, the rook is more sociable. It flies in large and ragged flocks and feeds communally in fields. Too wary to be a common garden bird, the rook will visit if you have a quiet country garden near a *rookery* (breeding colony), especially in the early morning and where a tall tree gives it a safe perch. It visits rubbish dumps in towns.

Throat pouch
The bulging pouch (beneath the base of the bill) is used for carrying food.

VOICE The rook makes a raucous *kaah*. The song is a mixture of soft caws, rattles and cackles.

Untidy feathers around legs

Recognition
Unlike the crow, the adult rook has bare skin in front of the eyes. A raised crest highlights the steep forehead.

FEEDING Rooks eat earthworms and insects, such as leatherjackets, beetles and caterpillars, as well as grain, acorns and fruit. Nests of small birds are robbed. Like other crows, rooks hoard surplus food.
Bird-table Rooks enjoy feeding on hanging bones, fat and cooked meat.

NESTING The rookery is usually at the top of a clump of tall trees: nests are often built close together but one or two may be on their own. Each nest is built by both sexes of twigs, grasses and mud and lined with finer plant material. The male brings food in his throat pouch to the female when she is incubating.

Tree-top nests *The social life is based on the rookery, although young rooks flock and roost separately in autumn and winter.*

Nesting information Late February – June • 1 brood • 3–5 speckled, greenish eggs • 16–18 days incubation: female • 32–33 days fledging • 4 weeks until independent

---

Crow family *(Corvidae)*

JACKDAW
Corvus monedula
Length: 33 cm (13 in)

A SOCIABLE AND ENTERTAINING bird, the jackdaw can be seen in many towns and villages, where it nests in buildings and old trees. In northern Europe, jackdaws often roost in towns during the winter but commute each day to feed in the countryside. Bright button eyes give the jackdaw an air of sagacity – experiments have shown that members of the crow family are among the most intelligent birds.

Grey hood

Bluish sheen on black plumage

Recognition Jackdaws are smaller than the other black-coloured members of the crow family.

VOICE The sharp *tchak* is a familiar contact call, but there is also a *chaair* note that is given in flight. The song comprises a medley of *tchaks* and other notes.

Aerobatic flier Jackdaws are agile in the air, sometimes performing aerobatics, apparently just for fun.

Social life The jackdaw is a sociable bird. Flocks of jackdaws fly and feed with other species, such as rooks (when they can be distinguished by their smaller size and *tchak* cries) and starlings. Mated pairs of jackdaws fly together.

Glossy, black wings

Young jackdaw The juvenile bird (left) is a duller colour than the adult and shows less contrast between the hood and the body.

Thieves Jackdaws are notorious for stealing bright objects, especially glittering jewellery. The habit is immortalized in Richard Harris Barham's *The Jackdaw of Rheims*, a nineteenth-century poem that tells of the jackdaw that stole the cardinal's ring.

FEEDING Jackdaws eat all sorts of vegetable and animal foods, mainly cereals, fruit and insects but they also steal eggs and nestlings from the nests of other birds. They usually feed on the ground and, being less wary, reach food before the larger rooks and crows arrive at the scene and drive them away.

Bird-table The jackdaw comes into your garden or yard to take a variety of scraps from the bird-table or the ground. In the garden, it shows the same enthusiasm that it has when scavenging in streets and raiding litterbins in parks. Try putting out fat and bones, especially in the early morning when few people are about.

All that glitters The thief of the bird world steals an earring. Jackdaws occasionally steal inedible objects, particularly if they are shiny, for no purpose.

Ground feeder Jackdaws search on the ground among stones and logs for a variety of large insects, such as these ground beetles, which are a high-protein food.

NESTING Jackdaws nest in colonies, usually choosing holes in buildings or tree trunks as nest sites. They sometimes take over old nests of larger birds or build in gaps in dense foliage or even in the chimney pots of occupied houses. The nest may be employed for roosting throughout the year. Both the parents build the nest from sticks, often accumulating huge quantities of them, and line it inside with hair, bark, rags and other materials, mixed together with earth.

Nest-box A jackdaw will nest in a secluded, large enclosed nest-box (p.31).

Hunger A jackdaw nestling begs for food.

Nesting information April – June • 1 brood • 4 or 5 spotted, pale blue eggs • 17–18 days incubation: female • 30–35 days fledging • Time until independent unknown

∴ BIRD CLASSIFICATION ∴

The early naturalists devoted much of their time to putting wildlife in order. They gave plants and animals scientific names and classified them according to their relationships with one another.

When you start observing the birds in your garden, it is not always easy to sort out the different kinds. There seem to be so many small, brown birds – how are they related to each other? A greenfinch is very like a chaffinch, but are the finches close relatives of the similar-looking house sparrows? Ducks, geese and swans are clearly similar in appearance and behaviour but what about the relationship between jays, magpies and crows, or swallows, swifts and martins?

Zoologists and botanists use a system to name and classify animals and plants that shows the connections between them. It was devised by Carolus Linnaeus over 200 years ago. He gave all living things a two-word scientific name in Latin or ancient Greek – international languages. The first word always states the genus; the second word is the species name. For example, *Passer* is the Latin for sparrow: the house sparrow is called *Passer domesticus* and the tree sparrow *Passer montanus*. Sharing the same genus name means that the two species have similarities. However, the scientific name for dunnock is *Prunella modularis*. This shows that the dunnock is not closely related to the sparrows, and explains why its old name of hedge sparrow is inaccurate.

Linnaeus also grouped every genus with strong points of resemblance into families, and classified the families with broadly similar characteristics into orders. For instance, fieldfares, robins, blackbirds, and thrushes belong to the family *Turdidae*. Swallows and martins are grouped in the family *Hirundinidae* but swifts are in the *Apodidae* family, although they have a similar lifestyle. The *Turdidae* and *Hirundinidae* families, together with others such as the finch family (*Fringillidae*), are all in the order *Passeriformes* (the sparrow-like birds), which includes all the perching birds and songbirds. Swifts, with their different, four, forward-pointing toes, belong to the order *Apodiformes*, which contains the most aerial of birds.

The table of species opposite shows the relationships between birds illustrated in this book. You can learn some interesting things from this bird classification. For example, you can see that long-tailed tits are not related to other tits and barn owls are rather different from other owls.

Carolus Linnaeus *The Swedish naturalist, Carolus Linnaeus, originated the classification system in his* Systema Naturae *of 1758.*

· BIRDS IN THEIR FAMILIES AND ORDERS ·

ORDER	FAMILY	COMMON AND SCIENTIFIC NAMES
Pelecaniformes	*Phalacrocoracidae*	Cormorant (*Phalacrocorax carbo*)
Ciconiiformes	*Ardeidae*	Grey heron (*Ardea cinerea*)
Anseriformes	*Anatidae*	Mallard (*Anas platyrhynchos*)
Accipitriformes	*Accipitridae*	Sparrowhawk (*Accipiter nisus*)
Falconiformes	*Falconidae*	Kestrel (*Falco tinnunculus*)
Galliformes	*Phasianidae*	Pheasant (*Phasianus colchicus*)
Gruiformes	*Rallidae*	Moorhen (*Gallinula chloropus*), Coot (*Fulica atra*).
Charadriiformes	*Laridae*	Black-headed gull (*Larus ridibundus*), Herring gull (*Larus argentatus*), Lesser black-backed gull (*Larus fuscus*).
Columbiformes	*Columbidae*	Collared dove (*Streptopelia decaocto*), Street pigeon (*Columba livia*), Woodpigeon (*Columba palumbus*).
Psittaciformes	*Psittacidae*	Budgerigar (*Melopsittacus undulatus*)
Cuculiformes	*Cuculidae*	Cuckoo (*Cuculus canorus*)
Strigiformes	*Tytonidae*	Barn owl (*Tyto alba*)
	Strigidae	Tawny owl (*Strix aluco*), Little owl (*Athene noctua*).
Apodiformes	*Apodidae*	Swift (*Apus apus*)
Coraciiformes	*Alcedinidae*	Kingfisher (*Alcedo atthis*)
Piciformes	*Picidae*	Green woodpecker (*Picus viridis*), Great spotted woodpecker (*Dendrocopos major*).
Passeriformes	*Hirundinidae*	House martin (*Delichon urbica*), Swallow (*Hirundo rustica*).
	Motacillidae	Pied wagtail (*Motacilla alba*), Meadow pipit (*Anthus pratensis*).
	Troglodytidae	Wren (*Troglodytes troglodytes*)
	Prunellidae	Dunnock (*Prunella modularis*)
	Sylviidae	Goldcrest (*Regulus regulus*), Willow warbler (*Phylloscopus trochilus*), Chiffchaff (*Phylloscopus collybita*).
	Muscicapidae	Spotted flycatcher (*Muscicapa striata*)
	Turdidae	Fieldfare (*Turdus pilaris*), Robin (*Erithacus rubecula*), Blackbird (*Turdus merula*), Song thrush (*Turdus philomelos*), Mistle thrush (*Turdus viscivorus*), Redwing (*Turdus iliacus*), Black redstart (*Phoenicurus ochruros*), Nightingale (*Luscinia megarhynchos*).
	Aegithalidae	Long-tailed tit (*Aegithalos caudatus*)
	Paridae	Blue tit (*Parus caeruleus*), Great tit (*Parus major*), Coal tit (*Parus ater*), Marsh tit (*Parus palustris*).
	Sittidae	Nuthatch (*Sitta europaea*)
	Certhiidae	Treecreeper (*Certhia familiaris*)
	Emberizidae	Reed bunting (*Emberiza schoeniclus*)
	Fringillidae	Chaffinch (*Fringilla coelebs*), Goldfinch (*Carduelis carduelis*), Greenfinch (*Carduelis chloris*), · Siskin (*Carduelis spinus*), Bullfinch (*Pyrrhula pyrrhula*), Crossbill (*Loxia curvirostra*).
	Passeridae	House sparrow (*Passer domesticus*)
	Sturnidae	Starling (*Sturnus vulgaris*)
	Corvidae	Jay (*Garrulus glandarius*), Magpie (*Pica pica*), Carrion crow (*Corvus corone*), Rook (*Corvus frugilegus*), Jackdaw (*Corvus monedula*).

· INDEX ·

•ACKNOWLEDGMENTS•

Author's acknowledgments
Thanks are due to David Lamb for a guiding hand and to the staff of the RSPB, especially Ian Dawson, for advice and assistance during the preparation of the book.

Photographer's acknowledgments
Many thanks to Jane Burton for her help and encouragement throughout the production of the book. She took a lot of photographs especially for the book and provided many others from her library. I would also like to thank Gary Huggins for his enthusiasm and hard work in tracking down and photographing some of the more elusive birds. A number of people either loaned tame birds or helped me find places where birds could be photographed. I would particularly like to thank Yvette Cameron, Margaret Cawsy, Peggy and Tony Davies, Derek and Jill Mills, Malcom Sharp, Mike Smith, Mrs. E.G. Taylor, Jenny Tyson-Jones, and Carolyn and Michael Woods.

Dorling Kindersley would like to thank the following people for their help during the preparation of this book: Hilary Bird for the index; Ian Bishop and Michael Walters of the Zoological Museum, Tring for research on nests; Liza Bruml, Josephine Buchanan and Andrew Mikolajski for editorial assistance; Jane Burton, Tony Graham and John Woodcock for illustrations; Bruce Coleman Limited for photographs; Nick Harris for DTP

expertise; Peter Luff for jacket design; Maryann Rogers and Teresa Solomon for production; and Mustafa Sami for building the feeders and nest-boxes.

All photographs taken by **Kim Taylor** especially for the *RSPB Birdfeeder Handbook* apart from the following contributions:

Jane Burton 8l; 9cr; 39b; 43br; 44cr, b; 45cl; 50t, c; 51t; 52cl, cr; 67cl; 94 **Robert Burton** 25b; 75br **Peter Chadwick** 7, 33; 35b; 43c; 45cr; 47c; 49c; 58br; 61b; 69c; 71cr; 73cr; 88c **John Daniels** 69t **Geoff Dann** 83tr **Philip Dowell** 41br; 91c **Gary Huggins** 50b; 52b; 55b

Courtesy of Bruce Coleman Limited:
Jane Burton 32; 36b; 39cl, b; 40b; 42b; 45b; 47cr; 49b; 58bl; 59cl; 63b; 76t; 77b; 78b; 81b; 86b; 90b; 91b **Kim Taylor** 6; 9b; 11; 24br; 35t; 38br; 53cl; 55t; 57tr; br; 60t, b; 61t; 63t; 64c; 65b; 66l; 67cr, b; 68cr; 69b; 70br; 71cl, b; 72b; 73b; 74b; 75cr; 76b; 79b; 84cr; 85t, c, b **Roger Wilmshurst** 84b

Abbreviations: b=bottom, c=centre, l=left, r-right, t=top

The Royal Society for the Protection of Birds is *the* charity that takes action for wild birds and the environment. Supported by over half a million subscribing members, the RSPB is Europe's largest wildlife conservation body.